The Ripple Effect:

Grace-Filled HABITS

LISA OSTREIM

Illustrated by Mikayla Ostreim

Copyright © 2024 LISA OSTREIM

Two Penny Publishing
850 E. Lime Street #266
Tarpon Springs, Florida 34688

TwoPennyPublishing.com
info@TwoPennyPublishing.com

All rights reserved. This book or parts thereof may not be reproduced in any form, stored in any retrieval system, or transmitted in any form by any means—electronic, mechanical, photocopy, recording, or otherwise—without prior written permission of the publisher, except as provided by United States of America copyright law.

Scripture quotations marked (CSB) have been taken from the Christian Standard Bible®, Copyright © 2017 by Holman Bible Publishers. Used by permission. Christian Standard Bible® and CSB® are federally registered trademarks of Holman Bible Publishers.

Scripture quotations marked (ESV) are from The ESV® Bible (The Holy Bible, English Standard Version®), © 2001 by Crossway, a publishing ministry of Good News Publishers. Used by permission. All rights reserved.

Scripture quotations marked (NIrV) are taken from the Holy Bible, New International Reader's Version®, NIrV® Copyright © 1995, 1996, 1998, 2014 by Biblica, Inc.™ Used by permission of Zondervan. All rights reserved worldwide. www.zondervan.com The "NIrV" and "New International Reader's Version" are trademarks registered in the United States Patent and Trademark Office by Biblica, Inc.™

Scripture quotations marked (NIV) are taken from the Holy Bible, New International Version®, NIV®. Copyright © 1973, 1978, 1984, 2011 by Biblica, Inc.™ Used by permission of Zondervan. All rights reserved worldwide. www.zondervan.com The "NIV" and "New International Version" are trademarks registered in the United States Patent and Trademark Office by Biblica, Inc.™

Scripture quotations marked (NLT) are taken from the Holy Bible, New Living Translation, copyright ©1996, 2004, 2015 by Tyndale House Foundation. Used by permission of Tyndale House Publishers, Carol Stream, Illinois 60188. All rights reserved.

For permission requests and ordering information, email: info@twopennypublishing.com

Paperback: 979-8-9901524-2-7
eBook also available

FIRST EDITION

For information about this author, to book event appearance, or media interview, please contact the author representative at: info@twopennypublishing.com

Two Penny Publishing is a partnership publisher of a variety of genres. We help first-time and seasoned authors share their stories, passion, knowledge, and experiences that help others grow and learn. Please visit our website: TwoPennyPublishing.com if you would like us to consider your manuscript or book idea for publishing.

Praises for *Grace-Filled Habits*

"With honesty and relatable examples, Lisa takes us on a journey from shame and the need to perform to grace and reliance on God's power and ability to transform us. *Grace-Filled Habits* is overflowing with useful tools and practicality, but Lisa doesn't leave it at that. You can literally feel her guiding and coaching you through these principles with the humility of a friend coming alongside you to walk the journey arm-in-arm. It's more than a powerful story and information. It's a guidebook for walking in grace."

Michelle Tornetta, Fitness and Soul Coach

"If you, like me, have ever battled the voice of shame because you didn't have the willpower to maintain a behavior that you know is so vital to your well-being, this is your book! Turns out willpower has nothing to do with it! I learned that having grace for myself and getting curious about what was underneath my behavior was far more valuable.

I have been able to create and maintain two new habits that benefit my overall well-being. And I believe I can continue to add and modify habits by getting down to and coming back to my true why. I will take small and steady baby steps!"

Erin Pahre, MEd, School Counselor

"I love how this book illustrates how the true path to health and wholeness starts with God! I love how Lisa shares scriptures, personal stories, and her love for God to encourage readers on their own journey of *Grace-Filled Habits*. This book has been such an encouragement to me personally. I'm so excited to see how this book will encourage others in their health and walk with God!"

Heather Nolden, Faith and Wellness Enthusiast

"God sent this book to me at exactly the right time, I was feeling lost and unsure. I knew what I wanted to change and build in my life but no idea how to get there. I wasn't sitting idly by; I had already put three years into trying to improve myself and my life through personal empowerment, doing hard things I didn't think I was capable of, counseling, life coaching, habit work and loads of prayer. While these things were beneficial, I still felt stuck. It was like a roller coaster; sometimes things were going well and sometimes things were crashing around me. Then I was invited to read *Grace-Filled Habits*. At the beginning, Lisa states, 'I began to develop habits with a different purpose, to honor God with my life.' This too was what I wanted to achieve, but I wasn't doing that and didn't know what more I needed to do to see this come to fruition in my life. Certainly, I had changed some habits but what I was learning wasn't generalizing across the many areas of my life that needed growth and change. It didn't fill those needs because only God can do that. What I needed most was to have a deeper relationship with God in the context of change. In *Grace-Filled Habits*, I have found that the Christ-centered foundation of scripture, seeking God's character, prayer, and inviting God into my habit life has created real change with the help of the Holy Spirit in a way that I believe will be sustainable and will truly renew my mind and change my life into one that honors God."

Heather Hollingsworth, MEd, Teacher

"The way Lisa incorporates God into every part of life is the way God intended it to be. Through God, she has made it her life's work to show other women His intentions for their lives and it shows in every aspect of this book. Lisa truly wants women to know God's heart for them."

Robin Parker, Health and Wellness Coach

Contents

Foreword 9
Dedication 11
Introduction 13

Part One: Setting the Foundation 19
    Chapter 1   What Is Getting in the Way? 21
    Chapter 2   In His Gentleness and Love, God Saves 37
    Chapter 3   Discover Your Why 55
    Chapter 4   Small and Steady Wins the Race 69

Part Two: Building Your Habits 81
    Chapter 5   Spiritual-Growth Habits 83
    Chapter 6   Movement Habits 91
    Chapter 7   Nutrition Habits 99

Part Three: Pressing On 107
    Chapter 8   Fear, Failure, and Frustration 109
    Chapter 9   Your Habits, Your Identity 123
    Chapter 10   Moving Forward 133

Keep Your Momentum Going! 137
Notes 141
Acknowledgments 143
About the Author 145

"My flesh and my heart may fail, but *God* is the *strength* of my *heart* and my *portion forever*."

Psalm 73:26 (NIV)

Foreword

Many, if not all of us, can relate to one or more of these crushing conditions personally, or at best, we know someone who suffers from depression, obesity, eating disorders, isolation, hopelessness, physical ailments, and/or discouragement. People are being crushed under the weight of busyness, comparison, overwhelm, and many other weapons the enemy uses to keep us from living whole-hearted, Christ-centered lives.

Within the pages of my friend Lisa's book, you will find grace-filled steps to help you combat what the enemy has tried to steal from you. Lisa offers pieces of her own powerful and vulnerable story to draw you into the Father's arms, for this is where we must start if we will have any success at all in forming lifelong, grace-filled, healthy habits that contribute to the fruit-bearing, flourishing life God designed us to have.

"Let us hand Him our small habits and watch Him work. Let us do what we can and let Him do the rest. Let us release our expectations and watch Him multiply our habits."

Throughout the pages of Lisa's book, you will be encouraged to consider your core values and create habits that spur spiritual growth, movement, and nutrition. She'll teach you the science behind the chemicals released in your brain that motivate you through even the slightest, diminutive, yet grace-filled habit. Each chapter offers scripture, reflection questions to ponder and journal, a 30-day *Growth Habit Completion Chart*, and a special encouraging prayer.

Lisa sets the table and invites you, her *Dear Reader*, to link arms, discover your true identity and, ultimately, live your best life! "I am a daughter of the

King…" 2 Corinthians 6:18 (NIV paraphrased). If you are ready to make some healthy, long-term habits in your life, I encourage you to dive into the pages of this life-giving book with grace-filled expectations; you won't regret it!

Michele Tupen
Revelation Wellness Chaplain

To the chronically ill momma: I see you. You live somewhere between exhausted and grateful. Exhausted from the effects of disease. Grateful like no other since you know the value of life. Dear Sweet Momma, you are enough. Your small habits offered to God are enough.

This book is for you.

"In him the whole building is *joined* together and rises to become a *holy temple* in the Lord. And in him you too are being built together to become a *dwelling* in which *God* lives by his Spirit."

Ephesians 2:21-22 (NIV)

Introduction

In 2001, I had mastered my habits, or so I thought. I was an elementary school teacher who followed the bell schedule. I was in a Bible study that met once a week. I went to the gym for at least an hour every morning and I packed a healthy lunch for work each day. My routine was flawless. And then tragedy struck and I was completely lost. In a matter of forty-eight hours, I went from working out at the gym Friday, to my Master's program Saturday, to the emergency room Sunday.

I was sick. Life-threatening sick. End-stage kidney failure came out of nowhere when I was only twenty-five years old. My life was turned completely upside down. Suddenly rather than running on the treadmill, I was barely walking from my hospital bed to the bathroom. Rather than enjoying my homemade lunch, I was tolerating low-sodium protein shakes. And, rather than completing projects for my Master's program, I was learning how to read lab results.

This health trauma changed the trajectory of my life. I loved my career; teaching was my dream job. But, being sick forced me to take time off from work and reevaluate my life from this new vantage point. Almost losing your life tends to weed out what's really important. So, I began to develop habits with a different purpose—to honor God with my life.

After leaving my public school teaching career in 2016, I began homeschooling my daughters. Being home more allowed me to focus on how I could strengthen my daily habits. I now had regular access to sidewalks for daily walks, nutritious food in my kitchen, and a new schedule allowing me to spend regular time with God. This pivot in my life is why I am writing this book today. It's why I became a health coach. And it's why I am passionate about helping women transform their daily habits. Because, Dear Reader, your daily habits matter!

You may feel powerless when beginning a new habit. I have coached many women who began with such a mindset. You know what you want to do and you know why you want to change, yet you struggle with *how* to change your habits.

Your struggle can manifest itself in many ways. You might experience overwhelm, feeling frozen, or unable to begin. You may procrastinate by putting off the start date because you're fixated on perfecting all the details before beginning. Or maybe you remain in denial. Even though you know there is a problem, you just feel stuck and don't know how to get started.

Or maybe you struggle to maintain habits. You know what to do and you start immediately. In your excitement, you might even work on several new habits at once. But somewhere along the way, your motivation and willpower dwindle and your new habits become another failed attempt at change.

Dear Reader, where do you fall on the struggle spectrum? Do you find it hard to begin a new habit, or do you take on many big changes at once and become overwhelmed? Or, are you somewhere in the middle?

In the past, I found myself fluctuating between both ends of the spectrum, but eventually, I discovered how to develop habits in a balanced and effective way.

I am honored to lead you through this process of developing Grace-Filled Habits. It is truly my joy! As we say in Revelation Wellness, the ministry I am involved with, it's my "get to." First, I got to experience the power of Grace-Filled Habits through my own trial and error. Then, I got to grow my skills and increase my own education and training. And now, I get to pass on everything I have learned to my coaching clients and you, Dear Reader.

In 2022, I became a Certified Health Coach through the Institute for Integrative Nutrition. I'll never forget my oldest daughter's response when I told her about my new venture. She said, "I thought you already were a health coach, Mom!" I guess you could say this new title was pretty natural for me. This certification gave me the knowledge and skills to officially help coach people in their health goals.

Later that same year, I became a Fitness and Wellness Coach through Revelation Wellness. This certification taught me how to incorporate faith in God into all areas of health. Since then, I've continued to grow my skill set with certifications in intuitive eating, strength training, trauma-sensitive yoga, and gentle movement.

My health professional trainings have played a part in preparing me to write this book, but I have also gained critical training from God through my health trials. In coaching, I love to share my personal stories of God's providence in my life. I have not always been what others would consider "healthy." Some of that was completely out of my control (i.e., kidney failure). But much of my out-of-balance living was something I could improve upon, and this is where listening for God's leading in my life has been essential.

My trainings have provided excellent knowledge, but my life experience has provided me the love of God to share with you, Dear Reader. 1 Corinthians 8:1 (NIV) tells us, "We know that 'We all possess knowledge.' But knowledge puffs up while love builds up." The God of love is what motivates my coaching philosophy. Building you up in love is what you will find throughout the book.

Each chapter contains truth from Scripture, which I refer to as a focus verse. I encourage you to meditate on the focus verse. Try flipping back to it throughout your reading of the chapter. The focus on God's Word is part of this different way of developing habits. Since we are looking directly to our

Maker, Creator, and Father to guide us in how we care for our bodies, we must draw from His Word.

We will study and meditate on the truths of God's character. Getting to know God at a deeper level will create security. Building safety and trust is key to successful habit development. This trust allows us to invite Him into any habit He leads us to.

Another key component to establishing long-lasting habits is being crystal clear on why you want to make this change. As you move through this book, you will get to experience an awareness activity that will help you look within and determine your core values. You will come away with a new understanding of your unique reason for developing new habits. The "magic" happens when God leads this whole process, and you see His character woven into your reason for change.

You will learn more about the power of small, Grace-Filled Habits. This book is not about tackling large goals or overhauling your life. That's too overwhelming! Instead, you will focus on small, manageable habits given to God, blessed by God, and multiplied by God.

You will get to put all of your new knowledge into action! I will teach you how to create your own personalized habits that fit your lifestyle and flow from your deepest desires. Keeping with the promise of small, I will show you how to slowly and sustainably incorporate one new habit a month over the next 90 days.

You might need to reference Chapter 8 multiple times as you build your new habits. Consider this book to be a choose-your-own-adventure book! If you encounter fear, failure, or frustration at any point, skip ahead to Chapter 8 for a dose of encouragement.

For greater growth, I strongly suggest that you begin to build a support group. Find a friend, create an accountability group, or hire a health coach to support you through this process, which will increase your odds of success.

At the end of this book, you will find a powerful resource to use with a coach or group. This resource includes activities to deepen your learning.

One final note: I will address you as my Dear Reader throughout this book to remind you that we are in this together. I long to sit alongside you, encourage you, pray for you, and watch you grow, but since I cannot do that, I share my heart for you on these pages. You, Dear Reader, are why I wrote this book. So lean in. Read on. And trust that you are not alone.

Ready? Let's go! Let's dive into a new way of developing habits. Read on with expectancy and trust, Dear Reader. God is in this with us. Let God's presence envelop you as you plunge into the waters of Grace-Filled Habits.

Dear God, as I enter into a new way of developing habits, I invite You to join me. I long for You to be my foundation and the One who holds all parts of me together. For this to become a reality, I need You to dwell within me, God. Fill me with Your Spirit as I move forward with new habits. Amen.

• part one •

Setting the Foundation

"In his *kindness* God called you to share in his eternal *glory* by means of Christ Jesus. So after you have suffered a little while, he will *restore*, *support*, and *strengthen* you, and he will place you on a *firm foundation*."

1 Peter 5:10 (NLT)

What is Getting In the Way?

• chapter one •

I was eighteen months into my first parenting gig and I was rocking it. Routine, as usual, was the name of my game. Every morning I greeted my daughter with a morning song, something I started when we brought her home from the hospital. And each day, she eagerly awaited my entrance into her room.

One particular morning, I turned the doorknob with a smile growing on my face, singing the first line of our morning song, and expecting her usual greeting in return. But when the door fully opened, I stopped in my tracks. Rather than waiting for me in her lavender-colored crib, she was standing, feet planted firmly on the ground. Looking up at my open mouth and wide eyes, she gave me the biggest smile, full of pride and satisfaction. That morning began an entirely new phase of parenting.

Overnight, her strong, determined will developed and we were off and running! This transformation came out of nowhere. Whereas previously, she had been content being held in my arms, sleeping at nap time, and staying in her crib overnight, she now constantly asserted herself. Her old status of contentment had morphed into curiosity. Her bright toddler mind wondered, *Just what could I achieve if I stretch my leg as high as I can on this crib rail and hoist my body up and over? Oh, I can achieve freedom and independence!*

For eighteen months, I had parented in confidence. Through challenges with sleep and food sensitivities, I had found ways to meet my daughter's needs and felt such strength and competence in my role as mom. But as my daughter's personality and will developed, I discovered a new part of me as well: my scary mom voice.

When we first adopted our daughter, I thought I would always use the sweet, inviting, gracious voice that came so naturally with a newborn baby. A voice full of patience and gentleness, even melodious at times. Honestly, I had never sung as much as I did as a new mom. But, with this unfamiliar side of our daughter and my lack of experience parenting a toddler, I developed a new voice that sounded sharp, stern, cold, and even, regretfully, scary at times.

This scary mom voice came from a place of fear. I feared I was failing as a mother and since I had no idea how to succeed, a helpless, hopeless feeling came over me. And that's when I would use my scary mom voice. Eventually, I created many types of mom voices to fit different situations. A louder voice often meant I wanted more control. A breathless voice reflected my sense of overwhelm and desperation. A whiny voice anticipated that I was about to wave the white flag of defeat. I would try different volumes and tones until I got the result I needed or I gave up in exhaustion.

Suddenly, rather than living my idyllic parenting experience, I was trapped in regret at the knowledge that this scary mom voice was coming from me. My body felt tight and constricted when this voice was at work. Our home felt unpredictable. As the years progressed and my husband and I welcomed a second daughter into our family, my mom voice continued to be unpredictable. At times, my daughters felt scared. Honestly, I hated this voice of mine. I spent nights asking God to forgive me, seeking peace, and pleading for help for the next day.

By the grace of God, that scary mom voice didn't always have the final word. There were days when the gracious, inviting, sweet mom voice still poured easily from my lips. This voice came from a place of love. I used it when I felt supported and confident, so it was easy to speak with patience and kindness. I would speak words of encouragement while I waited as my daughters put on their shoes or slowly ate their breakfast.

Parenting in joy, my sweet mom voice reflected what was in my mind and heart. My body felt calm and secure. Our home felt peaceful. And, my daughters felt safe. I loved this voice and this experience of parenting. I would pray for more of that feeling in our home.

My voice fluctuated so much as a mom to two young daughters because my thoughts and feelings were often as up and down as a roller coaster at Disneyland! I was human; in fact, I still am. This up-and-down, tossed-to-and-fro way of living lasted far too long. It didn't begin to even out until I started to really know the One who does not fluctuate or fail.

Learning a New Voice

The scary mom voice and all the hopeless feelings that came with it pushed me to a place of desperation. That's when I finally started leaning into God more and more. And in that leaning, my up-and-down ways were contrasted with His stable ways. He gently led and healed me. He never rushed or condemned me. He spoke kindly to me. When I cried out for help with my scary mom voice, He answered with His tender voice of love and correction.

In order to learn God's voice, I pressed into reading His Word and studying His ways. I needed to be close to the One I wanted to imitate. In 1 Peter 5:10 (NLT), I discovered that God speaks kindly to us. "In his kindness God called you to share in his eternal glory by means of Christ Jesus." God calls out to us with affection, goodness, and patience. This was the voice I longed to use with my daughters, and it was the voice I so desperately needed to hear more of.

God's voice of kindness is what we are going after in this book. We will work hard to let go of our harsh, critical voice. We will learn to stop using it on ourselves and others. In its place, we will better hear God's sweet-like-honey voice. When your inner voice sounds more like God's voice, you will find yourself living in more peace, free of the scary mom voice.

"Shoulds" Getting in the Way

When my scary mom voice came out, it was fueled by a belief of what *should* be. These little humans in my care *should* sleep at bedtime, eat what I give them, be quiet and calm at the grocery store, and always get along with each other under every circumstance. I had an ideal in my mind, and as long as my daughters fit into that, my scary mom voice stayed under wraps. The problem was that nothing ever went completely as I thought it *should*!

In this book, I am offering you a different way of thinking. Only, it's not my way; it's the way of the Creator. God doesn't speak to us in *shoulds*. Yet, many of us carry around a list of *shoulds* without even realizing it. There's a very good chance that your *shoulds* have entangled themselves around you in a sneaky, barely noticeable way. Perhaps you have thought to yourself things like *I* should *eat more vegetables, I should read the Bible in a year, I* should *work out at the gym like my neighbor does, or I* should *enjoy running.*

Carrying around all those *shoulds* is like carrying a heavy load of disappointment on your back. You constantly feel defeated no matter what you do. My daughters were in a losing battle because they were not able to meet my expectations. I, too, was losing my battle with how I believed I should speak to my daughters. I knew what should be and I felt weighed down by that load of failure.

I needed a different way. Just as I believe you chose this book looking for a different way to make changes in your life. Rather than the voice of harshness, we need the voice of God. God's voice calling to you is kind. And because God, your Creator, knows you so intimately, He doesn't expect you to change on your own. He knows the abilities, gifts, talents—all that He has given you, things that only work properly when you are tethered to Him.

God's Steady Voice

As you grow in intimacy with God, you will begin to learn to hear His steady voice. He will gently show you how He longs to be your source of stability. He is immutable—a big word that means unable to change and accurately describes God.

In her book *None Like Him*, Jen Wilkin describes God as the God of infinite sameness.[1] Infinite sameness is so different than the drastic shift between my sweet mom voice and my scary mom voice. God isn't kind one minute and unkind the next. All of God's attributes are always at work and they do not change. When you read in Genesis that God is sovereign, He is always sovereign. When you read in 1 John that God is love, He is always love. When you read in Romans that God is kind, He is always kind. God's unchanging ways make Him the best voice to listen to for your habit changes.

Fully embracing God's immutability will be your foundation as you develop new habits. Holding tight to the truth that He will stay kind to you throughout your process of growth is radical and completely necessary for developing Grace-Filled Habits. His voice will not change.

Coming back to our focus verse for this chapter, 1 Peter 5:10 tells us that yes, we will suffer: "After you have suffered a little while, he will restore, support, and strengthen you, and he will place you on a firm foundation." Developing habits can bring on suffering. When I suffered as a new mom, my inner voice changed to my scary mom voice. But God's voice will remain kind, especially in your challenges and in your suffering. That is why it is vital that you embrace God's immutable kindness at the outset. God's steady kindness is the foundation for successful habit formation.

A New Foundation

Going completely out of my comfort zone on a mission trip to Honduras years ago taught me the importance of a solid foundation. With only one week to leave a lasting impact, our team focused our efforts in two places: teaching kids the truth of the gospel and pouring a foundation for a home. God gave us a direct order to spend our time on the basics, the foundation. Focusing our efforts in this way would leave something lasting for the people of this small town in Central America.

Building homes and starting habits have one important connection: they both require a strong foundation. My dad was a home builder for over forty years and he never would have skipped the vital step of making sure each home had a solid foundation. And you shouldn't, either! If you desire your new habits to last, then you also need a firm foundation.

As I write about firm foundations, my days in children's ministry flood my mind. I sing the song as I type away: *The Wise Man Built His House Upon the Rock*. This song was based on the truth in Luke 6:48 (NIV), "They are like a man building a house, who dug down deep and laid the foundation on rock. When a flood came, the torrent struck that house but could not shake it, because it was well built."

That song also clearly told the opposite result as well. The house built on sand could not withstand the rains. I would be willing to bet your foundation for habit formation in the past was not built on the kindness of God. The firm foundation of His immutability. The firm foundation of His belief in you. The firm foundation of His strength. Rather, based on your past attempts at habit change, I would guess it was built on shifting sand. The shifting sand of *shoulds*. The shifting sand of fear. The shifting sand of a critical inner voice.

How do I know? Because that was my way for many years. It turns out that scary mom voice actually came from somewhere. In fact, it very much resembled the nasty inner voice that kept me on shifting sands.

The Root of Your Inner Voice

In my early twenties, I walked around with a nasty voice ringing in my head as I powered through workouts every day. Imagine the coldest drill sergeant voice you can, and that is what my inner voice sounded like as it boomed in my head. It was the exact opposite of God's voice of loving-kindness.

The drill sergeant voice would bark orders in my mind, driving me to do more, more, more. A typical morning at the gym began around five o'clock and ended around seven o'clock. I would attend an aerobics or strength class and then run on the treadmill before heading out. I was always on time and I did not miss a workout. My outward behavior was fueled by my drill sergeant voice yelling orders to work out every day at a level that exceeded good health.

One day, as I stepped off the treadmill dripping with sweat, two fellow gym members came up to me to talk. This was a rare occurrence for me as I typically didn't stop my workouts for anyone. After all, this was a gym, not a social club—cue the drill sergeant voice! One of the women asked me, "What are you training for?" I looked at her in confusion. She repeated, "What are you training for? A fitness competition? A marathon?" I shook my head and told them I wasn't training for anything. Later, I thought to myself, *That was a weird question. Why would I be training for something? This was just my typical Tuesday morning workout!*

I worked my body from a place of fear. That drill sergeant voice flooded my mind with questions like, *What would happen if I stopped? Would I lose muscle or endurance? Would I gain weight? Would I ever be able to start up again if I took a break? Would I stop gaining the praise and approval of others for my intense workouts? Would I be labeled lazy?*

So, I pushed myself for months until, eventually, my body would resist, usually in the way of an injury from overuse. My aching knee would often get the better of my workouts and I would have to completely stop for a couple of weeks.

Along with the disparaging questions, the drill sergeant voice also made false claims such as, *People will think you are lazy if you don't wake up before dawn and push yourself to exhaustion. Your body will change if you rest. Others will become stronger and leaner and you will be lacking! Ignore feelings of weakness or pain! Just keep pushing! Tomorrow, you need to work even harder! These workouts will never be enough!*

Digging deeper into the root of my scary mom voice, I recognized a connection. My old drill sergeant voice sounded oddly familiar to my scary mom voice. Digging down a little more, I remembered the various coaches who spoke into my life over the years. My middle school basketball coach had a way of just looking at me, using no words, and I knew he disapproved. He hardly ever put me in the game and never said anything encouraging. As I reflect back, I cannot remember him offering any praise to my teammates. As a result, my team struggled with low morale, and our losing record reflected our emotional state.

Contrast that with my high school soccer coach. This team also had a losing record, but Coach Bill always gave specific encouragement to every player. He looked us in the eye, called us by name, and told us something positive as individuals and as a team. Coach Bill would host dinners at his house where, after eating a meal as a team, he and his wife would speak words of life over us as we talked and laughed; it was as if we were a family.

Which coach caused me to actually want to improve as an athlete? It wasn't my middle school basketball coach, who left me feeling like any effort I made was pointless and would never be recognized. It was my high school soccer coach because he believed in me and considered me a good soccer player. He saw me as strong and capable, so I wanted to learn, grow, and improve.

He Provides a New Way

The discouraging basketball coach, the drill sergeant voice in my mind, and my scary mom voice all fed on fear to drive behavior change. With each of those three voices, I was trapped, burdened, and in bondage to the lie that I just wasn't enough. I could never measure up. Buried in *shoulds*, I powered on even though I wasn't getting the results I desired. I needed a different way.

Since you picked up this book about habit formation, I imagine you also need a different way. You have just pinpointed something that has been getting in the way of your success with habit formation. You have a need. And thankfully, God has an answer for your need. The rest of 1 Peter 5:10 (NLT paraphrased) goes on to tell us that, "He will himself restore, empower, strengthen, and establish you."

Consider the difference between your own inner voice of discouragement and the voice of God restoring you, empowering you, strengthening you, and establishing you. Close your eyes and allow yourself to imagine what that kind of voice would sound like. What words would bring restoration? What encouragement would bring empowerment? What tones would bring strength? By listening to and believing the voice of the One who restores, our inner voice and our thoughts about ourselves can shift.

After getting so fed up with my own drill sergeant voice and scary mom voice, I finally gave God the microphone to relentlessly pursue me with His love and kindness. It's God's voice that now guides my habits. He is now the coach who sees me in His image. He looks upon me with love and calls to me. He is well-pleased with me. When He sees me just as I am, He sees me as His beloved child: restored, holy, and complete. I am free to move forward to change my habits as He leads me. God wants to lead you in that freedom as well.

Dear Reader, having God as your encouraging coach will transform how you approach your own personal habits. As you accept more and more of God's love and get to know His voice of kindness, you will find it easier to develop habits from a place of gentleness. And you will transform from a place of confidence and security.

I am so thankful for this transformation in my own life. Now that I am no longer beat up by the drill sergeant voice, I get to pursue habits from a place of freedom. For example, I *get* to read my Bible; I don't *have* to. When I sit down with my hot coffee, Bible, and journal, it is my pleasure. I am not earning any favor. I am not avoiding a nasty glare. I choose this act of obedience because I want to hear more of God's kind voice in His Word.

I get to exercise in a way that feels life-giving for me today; I don't have to. When I lace up my shoes and head out for a walk, I am grateful. I thank God for the breath in my lungs and the movement of my joints. On days that I am busy, sick, or in need of more rest, I get to choose rest from a place of knowing I am loved. Taking care of myself in the ways God leads me is a true gift from a loving Father.

I get to eat vibrant-colored foods full of fiber, nutrients, and sustenance—I don't have to. Eating a vegetable is not a punishment for last night's cookies! I don't force myself to eat a food I hate just because someone says it is healthy. No, I fuel my body from a place of knowing I am loved and valued.

When you embrace God as your habit-development coach, you will find this new approach feels freer because you do not have to prove anything. You are making choices from a place of abundance and not from a place of lack. Throughout the remainder of this book, you will follow the same process of habit development that God led me through. But before you begin building your habit-forming foundation, you need to be aware of something important.

The Reality of Suffering

I am about to be the bearer of a hard truth: Changing habits can be downright uncomfortable. It is expected for it to feel a bit weird for a while and you will likely experience some suffering as you adapt to the changes you are making. Yet God's never-changing kindness will empower you as you move forward.

Coming back to 1 Peter 5:10, we once again see that Jesus knows we will suffer for a little while, even when He is calling to us in kindness. Go back to the very beginning of the verse: "After you have *suffered* for a little while..." (emphasis added). We cannot make change without suffering. But there is good news! Keep reading that verse to see God's promise as a result of your suffering: Jesus will *restore, empower, strengthen, and establish you*.

Prior to reading this chapter, did the thought of habit change make you want to run? Maybe your past suffering in this area made you want to avoid creating new habits. But as you continue through this book, you will realize more and more how much God is for you and how that understanding will get you through temporary suffering. With God as your foundational coach speaking life into you, you will move forward with habit development in confidence.

Now that I have spent many years allowing God to speak life into me, my inner drill sergeant voice is healing, which, in turn, is causing my scary mom voice to heal. With God downloading His truth into my mind and heart, I am healing.

Dear Reader, you will find freedom from trying to earn love and instead find healing by embracing God's love. As you lean in to hear more of God's voice of love, kindness, and encouragement, you will be able to press on. You will find strength. You will find healing. And you will find your new habits.

I can't wait to continue this journey with you.

Dear God, I am grateful for Your kindness. To be honest, I am scared to suffer. I am scared of the changes you may call me to. Help me to trust in Your kindness. Help me to lean into Your restoration, support, and strength. Lord, may You forever be my firm foundation. Amen.

Reflection Questions

How would you describe your inner voice? Give it a name or a label. E.g., drill sergeant, Eeyore (pessimistic), Piglet (timid, fearful).

_____

_____

_____

_____

_____

_____

How has your inner voice hindered and how has it helped your past attempts at new habit development?

_____

_____

_____

_____

_____

_____

How would you like your inner voice to sound? Is there someone in your life that speaks that way? What type of inner voice would be helpful as you develop habits? Get specific.

"Come to me, all you who are weary and burdened, and I will give you *rest*. Take my yoke upon you and learn from me, for I am *gentle* and *humble* in heart, and you will find rest for your souls. For my yoke is *easy* and my burden is *light*."

Matthew 11:28–30 (NIV)

In His Gentleness and Love, God Saves

• chapter two •

The tears would not stop. I couldn't catch my breath. Alone in my room during my senior year of college, I was at the end of myself. It turned out that rock bottom was a real thing, and I found myself there. The attempts to relieve my pain flashed through my mind: workouts, relationships, striving for perfect grades, and numbing with alcohol. Everything I had tried only added to my pain. There was an eternal ache within me that grew deeper with each strained breath.

Dropping from my bed to the floor, I couldn't get low enough. The lower I got, the humbler and more desperate I became. I was done being strong and independent. Thoughts of pointlessness and hopelessness raced around in my mind. *Raw*. I felt open and raw, and that scared me. All my facades of strength had been ripped away and I found myself in my truest state: Weak. Alone. Needy.

When I look back on that night, I can see that I was at a crossroads. I was considering how I could leave this earth so that I could be free of the pain that haunted me, but I also became aware that there may be a path I had never traveled. A different path of hope and healing. That hint of hope was what brought my attention outside myself.

In that moment, I knew I couldn't escape the darkness alone. So I called my counselor. She wisely pointed me toward a Higher Power. I hung up the phone and knew my next step. With all my heart, I knew God was my only hope. I had never cried a more sincere plea until that very moment.

"God, help me! Help me! Help me!" I sobbed over and over again.

The relief I experienced that night was sleep. Deep, restful, restorative sleep. The Holy Spirit had found His home in my raw, open heart. God gifted me with rest and the loving assurance that I wasn't alone. Never before had I experienced a calm presence like when the Holy Spirit entered into my life and rescued me in the kindest way. He brought peace to my weary, aching soul.

The moment I prayed, "God, help me," I received healing. Truly, overnight, many aspects of my healing happened. I woke up the next morning and the desire for alcohol was gone. My hopelessness had turned into hopefulness about my future. This new relationship and understanding of God's love and gentleness even transformed my daily habits. My everyday life looked different.

This was my first experience with God, and it left me hungering for more. In His great love, God met me right where I was that night. He brought me the peace and hope I so desperately needed. Knowing that God saw me in my lowest state and was with me made me feel more loved than I had ever felt before.

But it took more time and more trials before I learned to rely on God to lead me day by day. God gave me this beautiful experience on my darkest night to teach me about His character. Over the years, He also gave me two powerful Bible verses to deepen my understanding of His love and gentleness. We will unpack Matthew 11:28–30 and Zephaniah 3:17 as we journey through this chapter.

Through personally experiencing God's love for me and learning more in His Word, I have been able to establish life-enhancing daily habits. These daily habits serve to illustrate more and more of God's love and gentleness. No longer is pressure from the drill sergeant driving my habit development. Instead, the loving person of God is guiding my habits.

Dear Reader, I pray that you, too, will hunger for more of God and the gentle way He transforms through His Word. And as you receive God's love and gentleness, you will be able to develop your own daily habits that enhance your life.

God's Gentleness Revealed in His Word

That dark, desperate night ushered in the Holy Spirit. Immediately, I felt different and acted differently. Yet, my healing wasn't complete. What I lacked was God's Truth in my mind and heart. I needed the Bible to show me who God was. While entering into this new relationship with God, the blueprint of His Word was necessary.

I just didn't know it yet.

Maybe this is you, Dear Reader. You had an encounter with God or even many encounters with God. You have occasionally opened God's Word and tasted what is good and true and right, but you haven't quite recognized your need for His Word. The guidance and refining power of the Bible hasn't yet become a source of healing for you.

Or maybe you have experienced the transformative work of God's Word in some areas of your life. Now it's time to apply the power of God's Word to your habits. My prayer is that in applying the truths in God's Word to your habit formation, you will experience more of the fullness of God. You will see that He is interested in every aspect of your life. Dear Reader, as you get to know Him more and more, you will find strength in His Word.

The Word of God is living. When we ask God to help us understand His Word, He reveals truth. Because of this, the way we read the Bible today may not be exactly the way we understand it tomorrow. I've experienced this in my own life, especially in my evolving understanding of this chapter's focus verse, Matthew 11:28-30: "Come to me, all you who are weary and burdened, and I will give you rest. Take my yoke upon you and learn from me, for I am gentle and humble in heart, and you will find rest for your souls. For my yoke is easy and my burden is light." Reading this passage when I was a new believer, my eyes just skimmed across the words. I tried to connect with how a burden could possibly be light, but I failed.

Years later, God brought these verses back to me when I was asked to include them in a Christian fitness class with Revelation Wellness. The class combined stretching and strength work, a format that lent itself well to the paradox of rest and work found in Matthew 11. God revealed powerful truth to me as I studied those verses. And that truth transformed my understanding of how to form healthy habits.

God's Gentle Invitation to Rest

This passage starts with an invitation: "Come to me." That is what I experienced the night I hit rock bottom. I came to Jesus, and He met me there. The words of Matthew 11 connected to my salvation story. I had read those three words, "Come to me," many times, but now I was finally getting it!

When I returned to these verses as I prepared for my fitness class, I could hear the gentleness in Jesus' personal invitation. He truly desired the weary and burdened to draw close to Him. He knew He had what they needed, that they'd find true relief in Him. God had shown me back in my college dorm room that I could come to Him in my weariness, weighed down by many burdens, in bondage to my pain. Now He showed me that I could continue to come to Him. My needs were different now, but I remained a member of the *weary and burdened* people group Jesus addressed in Matthew 11. Jesus was still gently speaking to me. This connection allowed me to long for the remaining words in the verse instead of just glossing over them.

Reading with fresh eyes, I saw that Jesus didn't just promise rest; He personalized that promise: "I will give *you* rest."

Note that He offers rest. Not a to-do list. Not a ten-step process. Not a shaming message. No, in His gentleness, Jesus gives rest. On my darkest night, Jesus gave me rest. And as you, Dear Reader, come to Him, He will give you rest.

God desires rest for you. He knows what He offers is truly best. This is the God who loves you so dearly and knows your shoulders ache under the weight of the world.

I could have avoided years of achy shoulders had I understood Jesus' gift of rest earlier on. But because of my struggle, I have something to share with you now as you prepare to make your own lifestyle changes. If you are prone to strive, work, and toil—and may even have lost sight of God's design for rest—this book is for you.

Before we continue, I would like to take a pause for a moment and dispel any shame that you might be feeling. Shake off any shame! There is no shame if you have misunderstood rest for many years. No shame if rest and all the synonyms for it sound and feel like a foreign language. No shame if you have been skimming the words of Jesus, not able to connect them to your life.

Know that Matthew 11:28-30 is for you. Dear Reader, you are loved and God gently gives you rest. Let's inhale—slow and deep—and exhale. Do that again and again, until your shoulders feel soft, your breath is relaxed, and you are open to truth.

I believe that God wants you to continue forward from a place of rest. Begin by coming to Jesus and receiving rest before moving forward with your new habits. This is the way of gentleness. This is God's way.

God's Gentle Yoke

After Jesus calls us to Him for rest in verse 28, we come to verse 29, which is where it gets a little weird: "Take my yoke upon you and learn from me"…What? Jesus, what? Dear Reader, are you with me in imagining an egg yolk on you and Jesus? And wondering how that would or could provide rest? It just sounds like a mess needing to be cleaned up!

By skimming God's Word, I had missed something vital in this verse. Yoke is not yolk! Jesus tells us to take His Y-O-K-E: a wooden crosspiece that is fastened over the necks of two oxen or horses and attached to the heavy plow or cart that they are to pull. Rather than being separately tethered to the load, they are connected to one another with a yoke and then attached to the cart. This creates balance and causes each animal to pull an equal amount.

The idea of a yoke can make this passage challenging to understand. After all, the work that is involved with a yoke doesn't seem to correlate with rest. This is weird, Jesus. Work and rest are antonyms.

I needed God to show me what these words meant. And God did just that, giving me a tangible example in order to learn.

Since I was applying this passage to my fitness class, I decided it was time to put my Bible and notes aside and start working on the moves I would guide my students through. After I stretched and took breaths to warm up, I picked up my weights and began the workout. The weights felt heavy in my grip. I wanted to release them as I moved through the workout. Instead of giving up, I came back to the focus of my teaching.

That's when it hit me: I was working and I was in need of rest in the work! God showed me the application right then and there. As my muscles felt burdened beneath the weight of my dumbbells and sweat began to bead on my forehead, I called out to God, "Partner with me; yoke with me, Father!" With His Word so close to my heart, I felt His reply. "I am here in the rest *and* in the work. Come to me!" He didn't tell me to stop my work; He told me to partner with Him and that's how I would find rest.

This experience has stayed with me for years and it is cemented in my heart. Even after planning one hundred classes since that day, I have not forgotten that one. Why? Because of the stark contrast between this gentle leading of Jesus and my old drill sergeant voice.

In the past, it was the shame, criticism, and pressure of my drill sergeant voice that droned on in my head during a workout. When my weights were heavy, the drill sergeant shouted, "You are weak and alone. Don't let anyone see your weakness. Keep going!" That contrasts sharply with how Jesus leads and coaches me. He tells me to yoke with Him because He is with me and that rest is always available when I remain close to Him.

Jesus' gentle leading is also different from my scary mom voice. The scary mom voice often beat me down with *shoulds*: "You should be able to lift these heavy weights. You should not be so tired. You should be able to do this workout in your own strength." Jesus' gentleness in this teaching was so different from my old voices that I paused my class preparation to let the truth sink in. Jesus is not harsh, rude, or frightening. Jesus is gentle.

How could I expect to coach and encourage other women well without knowing firsthand the gentleness and humility of Jesus? I certainly would not want to spread around more of the drill sergeant or scary mom to the precious women God has given me to coach. No, I needed to lean in more and more to God's Word.

So I pressed on in my study of Matthew 11 and came to the second half of verse 29, which tells of Jesus' character. "For I am gentle and humble in heart." I believe this entire portion of Scripture speaks to Jesus' gentleness, but just in case there was any doubt, He gave us the reassurance that He is, in fact, gentle and humble.

God's Gentleness Is for You

Dear Reader, God gently invites you to yoke with Him and rest in Him. As your pressuring inner voice quiets, you too, will experience rest. As you lean in closer to God's Word, you will find rest in knowing you are not alone. God will give you deep soul-satisfying rest.

Reading further, we come to verse 30, where Jesus says, "For my yoke is easy and my burden is light." This is where we can truly breathe a sigh of relief. We know that Jesus, our humble, gentle teacher, calls us to Him for rest. And the result is a lightened load. We are connected to Him under the burden of work, under the burden of our calling, and under the burden of any struggle we face.

When this truth of Matthew 11 caught my attention, it reminded me of that first night I cried out to God and the resulting changes He immediately made. At that moment, the blinders were removed from my eyes and the reality that I was not alone was revealed. And, now with this understanding of Jesus' design for rest, I experienced the reality of Jesus' gentleness, His partnering power, and His sustaining strength.

Jesus revamped my understanding of Matthew 11. I discovered the truth that I do not need to strive. Instead, He wants me to be so connected with Him in my work, my marriage, my parenting, my friendships, my ministry, my exercise, my nutrition, and my everyday life in this dark world that I am no longer weighed down with burden. Rather than being a striver working in my own strength, I am to be a partner with Jesus. Dear Reader, can I get an amen?

I think many of us strivers look at rest as a good idea for others and only consider it one-dimensionally. To us, rest equals taking a break, a day off, quitting. But what if we have been missing the true meaning? What if Jesus' promise to us in Matthew 11 is for rest *in* our work? What if He is calling us to remember His Holy Spirit within us? What if He is calling us to remember His name: Emmanuel, God with us?

Applying the truth of Jesus' gentleness to habit formation will take the pressure off you. Suddenly, it feels possible to be blessed through a new habit because you are *yoked* to your gentle, humble Teacher. You are not alone, Dear Reader. You are working alongside and tethered to your Savior, who is near you and for you! He desires good for you. And He has a future filled with hope in store for you, friend.

Let God's gentleness lead you and you will find rest in your Grace-Filled Habits. God provides the perfect amount of both gentleness and love as we lean into Him. It's His plan for salvation as well as for our everyday life. Carrying both gentleness and love with you as you move forward in creating new habits will transform your life.

God Is Love

> "The LORD your God is with you, the Mighty Warrior who saves. He will take great delight in you; in his love he will no longer rebuke you, but will rejoice over you with singing."
>
> Zephaniah 3:17 (NIV)

I paused my podcast and stopped walking. A smile lifted my lips and I shook my head, marveling at what I just heard on my friend's podcast: God delighted in me, just as I was, right at that moment. He wasn't wishing I was walking faster or even running. He wasn't wishing I had coordinated my outfit better. Nope. He was delighting in me with each step, and even when I stopped walking, He continued to delight in me.

When I left my house that morning, I had no idea I was in for a lesson on love. I thought I was just taking my dog for a walk. But God had other plans and used the podcast to transform my understanding of His love.

I had been living as if God's love was conditional: If I did well, then He was proud of me and therefore loved me. What I learned about God's love on this podcast was that it isn't conditional at all. The truth is that God takes great delight in me just as I am. This wasn't the first time I heard this, but it was the first time it made me pause, literally. No longer walking my dog, I found myself at a standstill. God had the floor, and I was ready for His love.

This is God's way. He got my attention and showed me this powerful truth. He wanted me to understand more about His unconditional love at this exact stage in my life, so He pursued me in this teaching on the podcast. He knew that I was treading dangerously close to the lie that I needed to do more to earn His love. As my podcast friend focused on the middle portion of Zephaniah 3:17, "he will take great delight in you," the truth finally reached me. I did not need to earn God's love! His love was unconditional!

For the previous seventeen years of my life, I had been incredibly busy and incredibly purposeful in my role as a mom. But at this point, my daughters were both well into their teenage years. Homeschooling them was drawing to a close, and I was wondering what my new purpose would be. With that wondering, the old drill sergeant voice returned, shouting at me to do more and work harder. That drill sergeant really didn't understand the meaning of unconditional love! So there I was, about to buy into the lie that I needed to earn God's love.

During this transitional time, I struggled with a lack of purpose and sensed I was missing something. I felt insignificant, even unloved. Enter in the truth of Zephaniah 3:17a, "The LORD your God is with you, the Mighty Warrior who saves." God is with me. And who is God? The Mighty Warrior. And what is His purpose? To save!

Just when I needed it most, God, my Mighty Warrior, came in to save me from the lie that I had to earn His love. My thoughts shifted so I could imagine God, my Mighty Warrior, walking with me. So, although I may have felt insignificant, lacking, and purposeless, I was actually walking in step with my Savior. Powerful mind and heart shifts like this often take place on my walks with my dog through my neighborhood.

Dear Reader, I want to check in with you. Do the words "incomplete," "inadequate," or "insignificant" resonate with you? If so, I want to reassure you—you are not alone. I have stepped in and out of those places of lack. One of the most beautiful results of God's unconditional love is how it impacts your daily life, including your daily habits. Move deeper into the words of Zephaniah to find your place with God.

God has the most beautiful love for His people. "He will take great delight in you." It's mind blowing to think that He loves you and me this way. Why would He do such a thing? I don't do anything special. Of course, my dog would argue otherwise as she loves our walks! But, really, how could God delight in me when I just perform this mundane, non-amazing task of walking my dog?

Because of His great love. "In his love he will no longer rebuke you." And not only because He *has* love for me but also because He *is* love. God is love. I imagine God's name in the dictionary after each of His attributes.

Flip to the L section and find, Love: (n) affection, adoration, feelings of warmth, God.

It's so hard for us to fully grasp the truth that God is love, sovereign, immutable, omnipresent, just, righteous, etcetera. He is all of those attributes, all at the same time. So, He never is not love. God is love and that's that!

God flooded my mind with images of daily life: eating breakfast, taking my daughters to school, emptying the dishwasher, reading my Bible, and folding laundry. In all of it, God delighted in me. When I play another word in the game *Words with Friends*, God delights in me. When I binge watch a Netflix series, He delights in me. When I sit on the couch and pet my dog, He delights in me.

In all of that life stuff, He delights in me, and in *you*, Dear Reader. The remainder of the verse reads, "…but will rejoice over you with singing." Dear Reader, close your eyes and imagine the most mundane task you did today. Folding socks? Putting the silverware away? Hanging up your towel? Now imagine God expressing His delight in you by singing! Literally singing because He created you. He loves what He made. He is pleased with what He sees. And He rejoices over you.

God's Love Transforms

How can a message of love change a life? Specifically, how can a message of love help a person create better habits? As often happens for me, my example revolves around my dog.

When she sees that I have a treat in my hand, she immediately comes to me and starts performing her tricks in order: Sit. Shake. Down. Shake with left paw. Speak. Speak. Speak. She looks to me to see if she got it right. Not waiting for my command, just performing!

My dog knows what to do to earn her beloved tiny treat that she devours in an instant. She performs to get what she wants from me. Likewise, we tend to perform for God in an effort to receive His love. However, He tells us we've already got it! He says, "I am already with you. I already delight in you. I already rejoice over you with singing. Simply because I made you." No perfect performance needed.

This kind of love takes away all the pressure. This love removes the *shoulds*. This love quiets the drill sergeant. No longer do we need to worry about pleasing God because He's already pleased. The lies that more exercise, perfect nutrition, or flawless Bible study are needed are completely blown to bits!

Dear Reader, I have shared with you two Bible verses that have changed my understanding of God. By diving into His Word and seeking greater understanding, these verses have helped me to see God as He truly is. God's gentleness and His love will transform how you approach your habits, too. Know that nothing you can do will cause God to love you more because He already loves you perfectly.

You are now free to consider your habit formation as a means to simply enhance your life, not earn God's love. Walk forward in this calling towards growth as the God you seek sings a song of delight over you!

Dear God, I come to You weary and burdened, longing for your love. Longing for You to sing over me. Longing for Your promised rest. Help me to trust You as my humble and gentle leader, partnering with me. You are already singing over me! Thank You, precious Jesus, for carrying my burdens. Amen.

Reflection Questions

What positive thoughts and feelings do you have about rest?

_____

_____

_____

_____

_____

_____

What negative thoughts and feelings do you have about rest?

_____

_____

_____

_____

_____

_____

How could believing God is both gentle and loving impact your habit formation?

How might gentleness and love affect the longevity of your habits?

Journal a prayer to God. Share your thoughts, feelings, and emotions at this stage of *Grace-Filled Habits*.

_____

_____

_____

_____

_____

_____

_____

_____

_____

_____

_____

_____

_____

_____

"You make known to me the *path* of life;
you will fill me with *joy* in your *presence*,
with eternal *pleasures* at your right hand."

Psalm 16:11 (NIV)

Discover Your Why

• chapter three •

Karen was desperate for change. Fatigue and pain plagued her daily life. She was truly sick and tired of being sick and tired. The defeat in her voice was debilitating. Hopelessness could be heard in every sentence she spoke. In a last-ditch effort, she reached out to me for health coaching.

During our initial call, Karen said she was having difficulty getting things out of her lower kitchen cabinets. "It just hurts," she told me. "I used to walk during my lunch breaks, and now it hurts to walk to my mailbox. My clothes don't fit me anymore, and I have to buy new clothes. I need to exercise, but it's painful." These confessions were real and raw.

I felt her defeat deep inside of me as we continued through the health questionnaire. Dissatisfaction. Discouragement. Overwhelm. This heaviness hung over our call as we continued through the questions.

Karen and I worked together for several months. She was my very first client after completing my health coach training. Self-labeled as my guinea pig, she bravely agreed to work with me. Based on all Karen shared, I knew that regular movement would greatly improve her quality of life. Her goals aligned with this. She wanted to be able to play ball with her kids, take nature walks with her family, put on a swimsuit, and join her kids in the pool. Karen's motivation—her "why" for change—mostly involved her body performing and looking better in order to join her family in everyday life.

I took all this information and emotion into our next coaching call and set out to create a foolproof strategy for change. Together, we wrote out a one-month plan that spelled out the what, when, where, and how of her plan for movement. During each weekly call, we'd track how that was going.

The first two weeks went well. She was moving her body intentionally and feeling successful. She even began to notice that movement was getting a little easier every few days. But then her willpower started to fade and it seemed that everything and anything was getting in the way of her success.

Dear Reader, I am certain this result doesn't surprise you. We all can relate to the first week or two of a new plan that practically flows perfectly. During the first two weeks of a diet, Bible reading plan, gym membership, or walking program, excitement is high, and willpower is abundant. But then various "walls" materialize and progress slows or is eliminated altogether. Reader, when this happens to you, know you are not alone and there's nothing wrong with you, just as there was nothing wrong with Karen when her motivation fizzled. And there was nothing wrong with me as I became confused and even embarrassed as our plan "failed."

Karen and I were both depending on willpower to sustain her changes. *Merriam-Webster's Dictionary* defines willpower as the ability to control one's own actions, emotions, or urges.[2] Willpower is needed when setting New Year's resolutions. A Google search of the success rates of New Year's resolutions does not provide encouraging results. An article in Forbes Magazine stated that only 8% of New Year's Resolution setters maintained their goal for one month.[3] Drive Research published some disappointing results on their website. 9% of adults kept their resolutions all year long. 80% were no longer working on their resolution by mid-winter. And 23% of people quit their New Year's Resolution by the end of the 1st week.[4] Setting lofty goals does not seem to work.

The apostle Paul was well acquainted with the problem of willpower. Romans 7:15 (NIrV) says, "I don't understand what I do. I don't do what I want to do. Instead, I do what I hate to do." Sometime around early February, I have a feeling many of those who set New Year's resolutions are feeling Paul's words down deep. This whole process can be so discouraging and lead to even more challenges when trying to develop habits.

When we continue to fail, we begin to feel more and more discouraged, hopeless, and powerless than when we first set out to make a change. This is what was happening for both Karen and me. Karen's goals to lose weight, wear smaller clothing, and be active with her family were admirable. However, her ability to control her own actions, emotions, and urges was lacking. And my goal to help Karen may have been commendable, but I was relying on my own ability to control her actions, emotions, and urges.

What was missing? I listened to Karen's story. I tailored the plan to what would work for her schedule and her desired outcome. I provided accountability. I encouraged. I planned.

Feeling the burden heavy on my shoulders, I finally realized I was doing the work in my own strength. Watching Karen's growing defeat, I knew she, too, was trying hard to make changes in her own willpower. We were both falling short.

God had without a doubt called me to health coaching. I knew this was the work He had for me, yet what I was doing wasn't working. As He always has, He kept His promise to me to continue His good work. I told God all about my discouragement. As if He didn't know, I reminded Him that He brought me to this new career of health coaching. I asked Him to show me what to do, and in my weakness and shortcomings, God provided.

God's guidance came one day during a fitness class I was taking. The Christian fitness instructor mentioned the ministry Revelation Wellness and the program they had to train up Fitness Teacher Gospel Preachers!

That title alone intrigued me and immediately following class, I googled the ministry.

I began to devour all the Revelation Wellness podcasts I could, which revealed more and more truth about God's interest in every area of my life. I discovered what my health coach training program had lacked. God led me to Revelation Wellness and through them, He showed me that my coaching was failing because I was doing it in my own strength and willpower.

When their next session of instructor training began about two months later, I was in it. I have never looked back. I became the Fitness Teacher Gospel Preacher I had learned about during that one fitness class.

The training launched me into God's design for how I care for my body, mind, and spirit. God used our group Bible study in Nehemiah, vulnerable small-group sharing time, and the lead instructors' testimonies to transform my understanding of His deep love for me.

Little by little, I saw why my initial approach to health coaching failed. I didn't invite God in to be my "why." My "why" or my motivation had been to change my client's habits. To be their hero. To show them I knew the way to change their lives. If you are cringing right about now, I am right there with you. I am not proud to say this, but my why was *me*. I was my why. Yuck.

This realization was both bad news and good news at the same time. The bad news was that my pride had been stifling my client's growth. The good news was that God had removed my blinders and I could now see the truth. Once again, God showed me my need for Him and that He was close.

Upon completing my Fitness Teacher Gospel Preacher training with Revelation Wellness, God graciously brought me another client. In His humor and creativity, her name was also Karin. Spelled differently, but still … Karin. Listening to Karin #2 through a new filter, I heard her dissatisfaction with having tried all the different diet plans. (In hopes of bringing more clarity, I will now occasionally refer to Karen as Karen #1 and Karin as

Karin #2.) Disappointed in her up-and-down weight and fluctuating eating styles, she was done. As with my first client, I heard defeat in Karin's voice. But this time, I was armed with hope because God was in the lead.

I felt excited and optimistic when Karin and I met for our first coaching session. The look in her eye when I began asking her faith-related questions told me this was the way God wanted me to coach. I began with the question, "Have the diets you've tried led you closer to or further away from God?" Her shoulders softened, eyes lifted, and mouth quieted. As she considered her answer, her mind and heart began to shift. This time, I was inviting God into our coaching time together. This time, my questions went deeper than the surface. This time, Karin #2 was seeing what was lacking in her previous attempts to develop healthy habits.

When looking at Karin's motivation to change, I saw some similarities with Karen #1. Smaller clothing size was a goal both clients shared. But Karin #2 also had a deep desire to be comfortable with who she was. She told me she wanted to enjoy her life without making the focus be how she looked or what she would eat. Karin wanted a deeper relationship with God and didn't want that priority to suffer while she focused on her health.

For months, our coaching time followed a beautiful flow of focusing more on how God uniquely created her and less on what she ate or how many minutes of exercise she had completed that week. With Karin's why being centered on accepting herself and enjoying her life, she was able to discover more about who she was in God. It turned out she loved taking walks and stretching her body early in the morning before the rest of her busy day began. It wasn't hard to get up and exercise in the morning because God had coached her in creating that new habit. Karin discovered her new morning routine left her feeling invigorated for the day and freed up her evenings for group Bible studies and time with her family.

With each passing week, Karin connected more and more with how God made her and what values mattered most to her. When she pinpointed afternoons being a sluggish time of day for her, she knew she wasn't satisfied. As a school teacher, Karin valued being in tune with her students. So, she gladly made the decision to increase her water and protein intake mid-day, and her energy level increased. Not to lose weight. Not to wear a smaller size. Not to trick her body into feeling full. No. Her motivation was to be fully present for her students.

Karin was being coached and led by the Holy Spirit. Her motivation was fueled by the Almighty. And she was focused on what was truly important in her life. She flourished. She put the scale away. She stopped counting calories. She embraced who God made her to be. And she created habits that enhanced her life.

God had led Karin to His path, the path He had for her daily habits. Just as our focus verse Psalm 16:11 promises, He had made known to her His way that would lead her to life … not salvation, but a more abundant life. This new path for Karin, this new way of focusing on her health, led to joy and pleasure. And she was doing all this while walking closely with God, focusing on Him and His way rather than the scale or outward appearance.

Karen #1 and I were led or motivated by external ideas. A set of expectations that told us how we should live, or look, or be. We needed a better guide! Psalm 16:11 states, "You make known to me the path of life; you will fill me with joy in your presence, with eternal pleasures at your right hand." Without a strong guide, we were unable to experience joy or pleasure!

Two different clients. One with willpower, the other with God-power. One with short-term vision, the other with eternal vision. One with defeat and discouragement, the other with hope and satisfaction.

Dear Reader, when you look to God to show you your motivation or your "why," your habits will be led by Him. Let your "why" be your fuel for change. It may take some trial and error, and it will definitely require patience. But once you fully invite God into your process, He will guide you in the way you should go. He will provide your "why." "You make known to me the path of life." When we seek God, He will show us the way. So, let's pause and do just that: seek God.

I invite you to bring your focus to God now and pray the following prayer:

"God, thank you for creating me in your image. I want to invite you into this process of developing habits. Open my hands, heart, mind, and spirit to you. Take the lead. As you do, help me see more of who you made me to be. Show me what's in my heart, and make my motivation clear and pure. Amen."

Continue in prayer as you feel led until you are ready for the next step. To truly get at your most powerful motivation or your "why," you need to look within to what matters to you. A great way to do this is to determine your core values, which inform your beliefs. When I work with my clients, we spend an entire session on this. I'd like you to journey with me now into determining your very own core values. I recommend setting aside 30-60 minutes for this exercise. Take each step slowly and mindfully.

Discover Your Core Values

Step 1: Read over this list of core values.

Authenticity	Health	Love	Success
Community	Hope	Passion	Truth
Faith	Influence	Peace	Wealth
Family	Integrity	Power	Wisdom
Friendship	Joy	Recognition	
Happiness	Justice	Service	

Step 2: Read it over a second time and circle any words that feel important to you. Add and circle any core values that you feel are missing.

Step 3: Read over the list again and place a star next to ten of your circled values. Look for any words you circled that may sound repetitive. For example, if you chose joy and happiness, star the one that feels most true for you. Remember to check in with God when you are not sure.

Step 4: Repeat that process again to narrow your list to five words. Simply cross off the words you are eliminating.

Step 5: One more cut … this time, narrow your list to three core values!

Step 6: List your three core values here:

_____

_____

_____

Whew! You did it! I know that is a challenging exercise because every core value has importance. Keep in mind that just because you crossed off a word, it does not mean that value is not important to you. You have merely determined which core values are going to motivate you to develop your habits.

Step 7: Read your three core values out loud several times.

Step 8: Close your eyes and visualize how those three core values would play out in your day-to-day life.

Step 9: Write out your "why" or your motivation for developing new habits. Make sure all three of your core values are represented in your statement.

- Begin with the words "I will" and include the words "in order to." The following are examples from some of my previous clients:

- I will develop new habits that will increase my faith in God's love and provision for me in order to promote peace and balance in my family. (Core values: faith, peace, and balance.)
- I will develop new morning habits that will promote health in order to increase my ability to take care of my family and ministry responsibilities. (Core values: health, family, and faith.)
- I will establish a healthy morning routine in order to be my authentic self, love my family, and love God. (Core values: authenticity, family, and faith.)
- I will begin new habits that will increase my energy in order to have more joy, connection, and peace. (Core values: joy, connection, peace.)
- I will change my evening routine in order to improve my overall health and experience more joy and love with my family. (Core values: joy, love, family.)

Your Core Value Statement:

_____

_____

_____

_____

_____

_____

Dear Reader, you have just completed powerful work. This Core Value Statement is your "why" and will guide you as you continue through the rest of this book. I encourage you to write this statement on sticky notes or note cards and put it in various places around your home.

Your core value work invites God into your process, which will enable you to develop new habits and be filled with joy in His presence, just as Psalm 16 promises. Yes, this important work you just completed is going to lend itself beautifully to creating your new habits. But first, let's learn about how Grace-Filled Habits are different than any other habits.

Dear God, thank You for the unique ways in which You created me. Thank You for revealing my core values that lead me on the path of life You have for me. I am expectant and hopeful for all the joy I will experience as I walk forward in Your presence in my new habits. Amen.

Reflection Questions

Have the diets you have tried led you closer to or further away from God?

_____

_____

_____

_____

_____

Take a moment and reflect on how completing a habit, which is in line with your core values, could add to your joy.

_____

_____

_____

_____

_____

_____

Write about what this would feel like for you. How would your body feel? What words come to mind? How might your energy level change?

_____

_____

_____

_____

_____

_____

_____

_____

_____

_____

_____

_____

_____

_____

"Here is a boy with five small loaves of barley bread. He also has two small fish. But how far will that go in such a large crowd?"

John 6:9 (NIrV)

Small and Steady Wins the Race

• chapter four •

The crowd had multiplied in front of Philip's eyes. Sweat dripped down his brow as he surveyed the people listening to Jesus. The intensity of the message and the hike up the mountainside left the people groaning about their fatigue and hunger. Philip could not escape the grumbling. His own stomach spoke of hunger, yet he felt inadequate to meet everyone's need.

"Wait!" Philip stammered. "I have an idea! Let's buy enough bread so everyone can at least have a bite. That's better than nothing …" his voice trailed off as he began the calculations in his head. With his meager salary, it would take him six months to buy that much bread. The insufficiency loomed heavy. The magnitude of the task left him powerless.

Dear Reader, are you feeling powerless over your habits?

Suddenly, Andrew, another of Jesus' disciples, chimed in, "Look! There's a boy by the tree. It looks like he has lunch with him." Walking closer to the boy, Philip and Andrew determined he had five small loaves of bread and two modest-sized fish. Philip stifled a laugh at this absurd attempt at a solution to feed about 5,000 people.

The crowd continued to grumble about their hunger and everyone's patience was wearing thin. Jesus made eye contact with the boy and offered a smile of assurance. Motioning to the people to sit down, he called the boy over. The young boy loosened his grip on his meal and extended the bread and fish to Jesus. Again, a smile lifted the corner of Jesus' lips as he took the small lunch sacrificed by the boy, raised it into the air, and prayed to the Father, "Thank you for providing for us! Bless this meal."

Reader, God is providing for you now. Look for His provision.

Quickly transitioning from prayer to action, Jesus began distributing bread and fish to all those around him, walking up and down the rows of people, serving each person until all had been fed. The hungry grumbles quickly became sighs of contentment.

"Philip, Andrew, all of you," Jesus called. "Take these baskets and gather all of the leftover food. Do not waste anything!"

From this account in John 6, we see that the need that day was great (about 5,000 hungry men). The young boy had only a small sacrifice to bring, yet that modest offering was brought to Jesus. The Multiplier of small, Jesus, took what was offered and met the need. And there was food to spare.

Reader, what is God prompting you to offer up?

The loaves and fish stories in the Bible are perfect examples of Jesus' multiplying power. But those are not the only examples. Jesus taught that if a person has faith as tiny as a mustard seed, God can strengthen that enough to move a mountain! God's multiplying power is seen throughout Scripture, and it can show up in our lives, too.

Grace-Filled Habits are small habits offered to God. They are formed, fueled, and multiplied by God. When we feel maxed out, like we have little to give, overwhelmed and under stress, we can offer our small habits to God and watch Him work. Sometimes the smallness of our habits may feel absurd, just like five loaves of bread and two fish feeding a huge crowd. But let's never underestimate God's power in our small.

Dear Reader, just as the crowd experienced a very real need in John 6, you have a need. Your core value statement addresses your need. Your need may feel intense and daunting, but however big it may feel, God has the solution. By inviting God into your need and your process, you offer your habits to God for His power to work.

Small and Steady

Let us now learn more about small habits. Just as the young boy brought his lunch to Jesus, we will learn how we can bring our small habits before Jesus and watch Him work!

In his book *Mini Habits for Weight Loss*, Stephen Guise describes mini habits this way: "The ideal mini habit is always going to be at the level of lowest possible resistance that also begins the process of the target behavior."[5] I like to describe them as habits that do not create much push-back or resistance and can lead to more positive behavior.

Guise tells his own mini-habit success story regarding his desire to be more physically fit. Since he did not have an established habit for exercise, he began a mini habit of doing one push-up every morning. The idea of doing a single push-up every day did not create resistance in him. Once he was down on the floor to do his one push-up, it almost always led to more. He would usually find himself adding in some sit-ups as well, maybe even picking up his dumbbells for some bicep curls. His one push-up initiated the targeted behavior, which was to exercise and become more physically fit. Before long, he was regularly completing a 30-minute workout.

This example may not convince you that small habits can actually lead to big changes for *you*. So, let's look at the opposite approach. Instead of mini habits, what happens when you focus on *big* habits? This approach is highlighted in the long-running reality TV show, *The Biggest Loser*, in which contestants competed to see who could lose the most weight.

The Biggest Loser contestants faced big changes to their lifestyles. For those fortunate enough to be selected for the show, their whole lives were turned upside down for a few months as they left their homes, families, jobs, and communities to join the other contestants and trainers at the training facility. They also underwent big changes in what they ate and how many calories they consumed. Twice-a-day workouts were introduced to their schedule as well.

Admittedly, I was one of the biggest fans of *The Biggest Loser*. Season after season, I remained a close follower of the show. I faithfully cheered on my favorite contestants. After all the improvements to their overall health were made at the end of each season, I dreamed of how they would go on to live lives full of energy, vitality, health, and joy.

Boy, was I ever disappointed to learn my dream was not reality. But if I was disappointed, imagine how terrible the hard-working contestants must have felt. Rather than achieving big, long-lasting results, one study showed that thirteen out of fourteen contestants regained the weight after six years.[6]

Big, drastic changes are hard to maintain, and they often lead to burnout. Small changes, however, are more likely to lead to long-term habits, which then lead to success. There is amazing science behind why small changes are so effective … and it all starts in your brain.

Chemical Surge Leads to Success

Dopamine is a chemical released in your brain that makes you feel good and aids in motivation. When creating habits, it is important to access and fuel that God-given chemical as much as possible. *The Harvard Business Review* states, "Your brain releases dopamine when you achieve goals. And since dopamine improves attention, memory, and motivation, even achieving a small goal can result in a positive feedback loop that makes you more motivated to work harder going forward."[7]

It's much easier to fuel dopamine with small habits than large ones. For example, whenever my client, Amy, completed her Grace-Filled Habit of putting on her running shoes each day and walking to her mailbox, her brain sent a rush of dopamine, telling her she was successful. Her motivation surged and she was excited to meet her goal again the next day.

Contrast that with a non-runner whose goal is to run a mile every day. She heads out the door, runs a block, feels winded, heads for home, and experiences a sense of discouragement and even embarrassment for not meeting her goal. She feels like a failure. Rather than a boost of the feel-good chemical, dopamine, her brain actually releases the stress hormone, cortisol. Cortisol can lead to unwanted symptoms such as increased anxiety, weight gain, and trouble sleeping.

When my client, Sara, began reading one Scripture verse and journaling for a few minutes each morning, she felt successful. Dopamine surged in her brain, which motivated her to continue. Contrast that with a person who sets out to read the Bible in a year and finds they are ten chapters behind by the second week of reading. Cortisol floods the brain and they give up.

Dear Reader, are you feeling this? When thinking about your past attempts at creating habits, did you ever find yourself feeling worse than when you first set out to make a change? You were not imagining things! Setting big goals and not succeeding has put your brain and body in a tough place. Discouragement has had its way. But no more! You are on a new path. And this path is going to flood your brain with dopamine and messages of hope. You are now going to work with God and the way He created your brain.

Discouragement often gets in the way of successfully sticking with habits. That old drill sergeant creeps in again and has her way. "You said you'd be running a mile today, and look, you couldn't even make it two blocks." Who wants to face that downer? It feels better to just stick to the old way than face that drill sergeant's discouragement.

Instead of the drill sergeant who always shouts, pressures, and condemns, let's access Jesus as our coach. Let us hand Him our small habits and watch Him work. Let us do what we can and let Him do the rest. Let us release our expectations and watch Him multiply our habits.

Create a Plan for Your Grace-Filled Habit

Habits don't just happen; effort is required. And putting in the effort upfront will help your habit become successful.

You have already done the big work of looking at why your past habits didn't stick, learning to focus on God as the best coach with His gentleness and love, and determining your unique core values. This next step will seal the deal for your habits to become a success.

Now, it is time to think about your unique wiring for getting things done. Do you like to have a deadline? Or do deadlines stress you out? Keep this in mind as you decide when to complete each new habit you create. What time of day will you do it? You might schedule it into your phone with a reminder for that specific time. Or maybe you would like to anchor it to another existing daily habit or ritual such as when you wake up, brush your teeth, eat lunch, or go to bed. Or perhaps you prefer the flexibility of simply saying, "This habit will be completed sometime before I go to bed."

Another important part of planning for your new habit is preparing for and utilizing the help of the feedback loop. James Clear, in his popular book, *Atomic Habits*, explains "the four-step pattern of every habit: cue, craving, response, reward. These steps are versatile across many types of habits and help to create success."[8] (See my website: www.empoweringhealthcoach.com for a fun, short video of my dog demonstrating these four steps.)

For this portion of your planning, you will need to determine your specific feedback loop. This may sound very technical, but don't worry; I will guide you through these four steps.

The four steps for creating a feedback loop, as stated by James Clear, are:
1. The cue–something that triggers your brain to perform your new habit. Make it obvious.
2. The craving– the motivation or desire that fuels your habit. Make it attractive.
3. The response– the actual habit you perform. Make it easy.
4. The reward– the end goal of every habit. Make it satisfying.

Example of this feedback loop:
- Cue: My running shoes are placed by the front door.
- Craving: I long to take daily walks and feel good about moving my body.
- Response: I put on my shoes and take a walk.
- Reward: My desire to become a walker is fulfilled as I complete my habit.

In the following three chapters, you will get to craft your very own personalized Grace-Filled Habits. You will follow the same format for each type of habit you create. You will work on creating habits in three different areas: spiritual growth, movement, and nutrition. In keeping with the promise of small, you will only be focusing on one habit at a time. This will help ensure your success and eliminate overwhelm. Refer back to this page whenever you need.

Format for Creating Grace-Filled Habits:

1. Read over your Core Value Statement.
2. Write a Grace-filled Habit that doesn't create much push-back or resistance and can lead to more activity.

3. Make a plan for your habit. When will it happen? Will it be attached to another habit? What do you need to have ready to implement your habit?
4. List the four steps in your feedback loop: cue, craving, response, and reward.
5. Write out your full habit, including the plan.
6. Test it against your Core Value Statement. Does your new habit support your Core Value Statement?

In part two of this book, you will put these 6 steps into action!

Dear God, I ask You to multiply my small! I feel I have little to offer, but this is not about me. You are the multiplier. So, I come to You, God, with my offer held out to You. I trust You, Father. You are good and so powerful. I can't wait to see the ripple effects of Your power on my small habits. Amen.

Reflection Questions

Write some reflection thoughts about your experience with big or small habit changes you have attempted in the past. What worked? What did not work? What were some of the feelings you associated with those big or small habit changes? (Helpful tip: Google the term: Feelings Wheel. Pick out 3–5 "feeling" words.)

_____
_____
_____
_____
_____
_____
_____
_____
_____
_____
_____
_____

What type of habit plan feels like it would be most successful for you? Choosing a specific time of day? Anchoring it to another habit? No timeline at all? Please keep in mind that this can always shift. The ability to pivot your habit plan is a good thing.

_____

_____

_____

_____

_____

_____

_____

_____

_____

_____

_____

_____

_____

• part two •

Building Your Habits

"But grow in the *grace* and *knowledge* of our Lord and Savior Jesus Christ. To him be *glory* both now and *forever*! Amen."

2 Peter 3:18 (NIV)

Spiritual-Growth Habits

• chapter five •

Let's go! You have made it to Chapter 5! You have done all the groundwork and now you are ready to start creating new habits. I am so excited for you as I know your new habits will be powerful and life-enhancing.

We are intentionally beginning our work with spiritual growth since, as we covered in Chapters 1 and 2, God and His Word play a vital role in successfully creating habits. The growth you experience from developing a new spiritual habit will lead to successful movement and nutrition habits.

Developing a deeper knowledge of God leads to spiritual growth. In our focus verse, Peter tells us how to grow by giving us an action step: grow in the grace and knowledge of our Lord. As you work through this chapter, you will grow in the knowledge of God as you practice your new spiritual habit.

Create Your Spiritual-Growth Habit

Use the following steps to create one habit to implement right away:

Step 1: Read over your Core Value Statement.

Step 2: Write a Grace-Filled Habit for spiritual growth that doesn't create much push-back or resistance in you and can lead to more.

Examples include reading the Bible for five minutes, praying for one person, reading the verse of the day, or listening to the Bible out loud for five minutes a day.

Step 3: Make a plan for your habit.

Create a place where your habit will happen; have your Bible, journal, or any other necessary items ready, and choose a time to do it. Be sure to make it enjoyable! Add in your favorite coffee, light a candle, or buy a pretty journal.

Step 4: Write out your four steps in the feedback loop.

Example:
- Cue (make it obvious)—I place my Bible where I'll see it every day.
- Craving (make it attractive)—I desire wisdom and direction from God's Word. (Don't forget the coffee, candle, or pretty journal!)
- Response (make it easy)—I read my Bible for five minutes.
- Reward (make it satisfying)—I receive wisdom for a current difficult situation.

Step 5: Write out your habit (including the plan).

Examples: I will listen to the Bible for five minutes each day while I make my breakfast. I will read the verse of the day before I get out of bed each morning. I will pray for one of my children each night before I go to bed.

_____

_____

_____

_____

_____

Step 6: Test your habit.

Does your new habit support your Core Value Statement? Does your new habit create resistance in you? Could your new habit lead to more?

Example: A habit of praying for ten minutes a day could create resistance on busy, hectic days, whereas a habit of reading the Bible for five minutes a day could lead to ten minutes.

Begin your spiritual growth habit today and track your progress for 30 days using the following chart. Enjoy the dopamine rush when you mark the heart indicating you completed your habit for the day. Celebrate! Pat yourself on the back. Maybe every five days you tell a friend about your success. Enjoy the process of creating a new life-enhancing habit.

No need to rush here. Please focus and give great attention to your new spiritual growth habit for the next 30 days, before moving on to the next chapter. See www.empoweringhealthcoach.com for a 30-Day devotional designed to accompany you through this phase.

Note: If at any point during these 30 days of working on your spiritual growth habit you find you are struggling with any fear, failure, or frustration, I encourage you to read Chapter 8 for encouragement and tips.

Habit Tracker

Each day you complete your spiritual growth habit, color in the circle.

Start Date: _____ End Date: _____

1	2	3	4	5
6	7	8	9	10
11	12	13	14	15
16	17	18	19	20
21	22	23	24	25
26	27	28	29	30

Now that you have completed 30 days with a new habit, you are ready to add an additional habit. Your next habit will be a movement habit. You will continue your spiritual growth habit as you build your new movement habit. But first, it's time for some reflection. How did the past 30 days go for you?

Dear God, I desire to know You more through daily interaction with You. Please help me grow in Your grace and knowledge. Holy Spirit, remind me of my new habit, daily. May You be glorified as I live more like You. Amen

Reflection Questions

What went well during these past 30 days? How did you grow?

_____

_____

_____

_____

_____

_____

What challenges did you face with completing your habit during the past 30 days? Did anything get in your way?

_____

_____

_____

_____

_____

_____

Journal a prayer to God. Share your thoughts, feelings, and emotions at this stage of *Grace-Filled Habits*.

"But those who *trust* in the Lord will receive new *strength*. They will fly as high as eagles. They will *run* and not get tired. They will *walk* and not grow weak."

Isaiah 40:31 (NIrV)

Movement Habits

• chapter six •

You have been going strong for 30 days with your new spiritual growth habit! Because God's Word is alive, active, and powerful, you are not the same person you were when you began this journey. You have read, prayed, or journaled your way to a stronger version of yourself. Now you are ready to add on to your spiritual habit.

For the next month, you will incorporate a new movement habit into your daily routine. Take a deep breath; there is no need to worry. This is not where I suddenly ask you to begin a 5k running program! We are still working on Grace-Filled Habits that are small, attainable, and dopamine-inducing.

Just as our focus verse states, you will begin with *trust in the Lord*. As you lean into God in your spiritual growth, you can trust that He will lead you to—and strengthen you to complete—a movement habit that He Himself has planned for you. By your trust in Him, you *will receive new strength*.

Trust that in your new strength, He will enable you to move. Whether that movement is running, walking, strength training, dancing, hiking, or stretching, do it with joy and thanksgiving! Smile! Offer thanks to God for any movement you are able to do each day.

I believe you could list many reasons why adding movement into your life would be a positive thing. Let me just share some of my favorite benefits:
- Helps with memory
- Improves mood
- Strengthens muscles and bones
- Increases heart health
- Improves insulin absorption
- Improves blood and oxygen flow

Create Your Movement Habit

Use the following steps to create one habit to implement right away:

Step 1: Read your Core Value Statement.

Step 2: Write a Grace-Filled Habit for movement that does not create much push-back or resistance in you and can lead to more movement.

Examples: Walk around your block, dance to one song, do one squat, or put your walking shoes on and step outside.

Step 3: Make a plan for your habit.

Examples: Place your walking/running shoes and activewear in a convenient place. Create a motivational playlist that helps get you moving. Choose a consistent time such as immediately following your spiritual habit, at eight o'clock each morning, or after dinner.

Step 4: Write out your four steps in the feedback loop.

Example:
- Cue (make it obvious)—I place my yoga mat and weights in my room.

- Craving (make it attractive)—I want to get stronger and relieve anxiety in my body. (Make it enjoyable by including a friend or adding music!)
- Response (make it easy)—I lift my weights and stretch on my mat.
- Reward (make it satisfying)—I completed my habit and moved more.

Step 5: Write out your habit, including the plan.

Examples: I will dance to one song each morning after I read my Bible verse for the day. I will do a push-up before bed each night.

_____
_____
_____
_____
_____
_____

Step 6: Test your habit.

Does your new habit support your Core Value Statement? Does your new habit create resistance in you? Could your new habit lead to more?

Example: A habit of jogging for ten minutes a day could create resistance in you on full days. A habit of walking for five minutes a day could lead to ten minutes.

Begin your additional habit today or tomorrow! Track your progress for both your spiritual growth and movement habits for 30 days using the chart on the next page.

As you complete your habits and receive that rush of dopamine, celebrate! Take note of the flood of positive emotions you experience with your success to help you continue in your new habits. Not to mention, the mood boost you are now receiving from moving your body! You are making your brain so happy!

Habit Tracker

Each day you complete your spiritual growth and movement habits, color in the circle.

Start Date: _____   End Date: _____

1	2	3	4	5
6	7	8	9	10
11	12	13	14	15
16	17	18	19	20
21	22	23	24	25
26	27	28	29	30

You have now completed 60 days of new habits! In the next chapter, you will add one more habit, specifically a nutrition habit. I am so excited for you as you go forward with your new habits. But first, some reflection time.

Dear God, my trust is in You. I ask You to give me new strength as I wait on Your continued work in my life through my habits. I believe You are working. I believe You are the source of all strength and ability. And I believe You never tire or grow weak. I need Your strength as I continue in Your transformative work. Amen.

Reflection Questions

What went well over the last 30 days? Did you gain strength? Did you smile while you moved? Did you find a new way of moving that brought you joy?

_____

_____

_____

_____

_____

What challenges did you face? What got in the way of your spiritual growth habit or movement habit? Are any adjustments necessary before you head into your next habit?

_____

_____

_____

_____

_____

Note: If you have been struggling while working on your spiritual growth and movement habits, take a look at Chapter 8. You'll find help with fear, failure, or frustration.

"'Everything is permissible for me,'
but not everything is *beneficial*.
'Everything is permissible for me,' but
I will not be mastered by anything."

1 Corinthians 6:12 (CSB)

Nutrition Habits

• chapter seven •

Our order for establishing habits has been strategic. You have now completed 60 days of your spiritual growth habit. In her book *Think, Learn, Succeed*, Dr. Caroline Leaf states that it takes 63 days to change an automated habit. So, good news! You are well on your way to hardwiring your spiritual growth habit into your brain. And you are about halfway to firmly establishing your movement goal.

I am well aware that everyone is different, but my hope is that because you have taken time setting yourself up for success, you now feel ready to add in your third and final habit. However, if you need more time to work on your spiritual growth and movement habits before adding another one, you have the grace and the freedom to do that.

Ready to incorporate one more small Grace-Filled Habit? Let's go! We are focusing on nutrition now, but we are *not* taking any foods away. Breathe in that truth!

Just as our focus verse states that "Everything is permissible," literally all foods *are* permissible. We are not suddenly switching up the plan here. You will not be asked to restrict calories, eat only celery, or go on the ice cube diet! No! You will only add a life-enhancing nutrition habit, not take any foods away.

I encourage you to focus on the truth that Paul shares in 1 Corinthians 6:12, "not everything is beneficial for me–but I will not be mastered by anything." I saved the nutrition habit for last because food can so easily become an obsession that attempts to master us! But, as you continue to include God in your daily life as you work on your spiritual growth habit, you will increasingly turn to your Lord as Master rather than being mastered by your nutrition habit. God, as your Master, is your food, your sustenance, and your focus! Your nutrition habit will enhance your life, not be master over your life.

You are wise, Dear Reader! I know you are aware of the benefits of good nutrition. Let me share a few of my favorites:

- Increased fiber (through produce and grains) helps with digestion.
- Drinking more water leads to better focus, energy, and digestion.
- Eating a variety of colorful fruits and vegetables can decrease the risk of cancer and strengthen your immune system.
- Colorful foods make meals look more attractive.

Create Your Nutrition Habit

Use the following steps to create one habit to implement right away:

Step 1: Read over your Core Value Statement.

Step 2: Write a Grace-Filled Habit for nutrition that doesn't create much push-back or resistance in you and can lead to more.

Examples: Eat a serving of vegetables each day. Drink a glass of water. Eat an apple a day.

Step 3: Make a plan for your habit.

Examples: Add a serving of fruit or vegetables with dinner each evening. Drink a glass of water first thing in the morning every day.

Step 4: Write out your four steps in the feedback loop.

Example:
- Cue (make it obvious)—I place a bowl of fresh apples on my kitchen counter.
- Craving (make it attractive)—I desire the sweet taste of the apples, and I appreciate the knowledge that I am fueling my body well. (Make it enjoyable! Use a fun plate or bowl.)
- Response (make it easy)—I eat an apple.
- Reward (make it satisfying)—I receive the nutrition the apple gives me.

Step 5: Write out your habit, including the plan.

Examples: I will put a glass of water next to my bed each night and drink the entire glass before I get up in the morning. I will slice up carrots each morning and put them in my lunch bag to eat at lunch each day.

_____

_____

_____

_____

_____

_____

Step 6: Test your habit.

Does your new habit support your Core Value Statement? Does your new habit create resistance in you? Could your new habit lead to more?

Example: A habit of eating a huge salad every day could create resistance in you on busy days. A habit of eating three baby carrots a day could lead to six baby carrots.

Begin your nutrition habit today! Track your progress for your three new habits (spiritual growth, movement, and nutrition) for 30 days. Each day that you complete your habits, you will color in a heart on the chart. You are experiencing the fruit of your habits, aided by your friend dopamine!

Habit Tracker

Each day you complete your spiritual growth, movement, and nutrition habits, color in the circle.

Start Date: _____   End Date: _____

① 1	② 2	③ 3	④ 4	⑤ 5
6	7	8	9	10
11	12	13	14	15
16	17	18	19	20
21	22	23	24	25
26	27	28	29	30

You have now completed 90 days of new habits. Congratulations! Right about now, I am longing to hug you, high-five you, pat you on the back ... something, anything, to say, "*Well done, Dear Reader*!" Humor me, please, by hugging yourself. Look in the mirror, smile, and say, "Well done!"

Dear God, sometimes I think I want restriction and control. But, You are a God of love. You give your people free will. So, help me, God. Help me to be so in tune with Your best, that I can clearly identify what is beneficial for me. That I would clearly see Your best and what You desire for me. God, may Your vision become my vision. Amen.

Reflection Questions

What went well over the last 30 days? How did your nutrition habit make you feel? Did you experience increased energy? Better focus?

_____

_____

_____

_____

_____

_____

What challenges did you face? What got in the way of your spiritual growth habit, movement habit, or nutrition habit?

_____

_____

_____

_____

_____

_____

How will you move forward from here? Will you print more 30-day habit trackers to continue tracking your three habits?
(Go to www.empoweringhealthcoach.com for more habit trackers.)

_____

_____

_____

_____

_____

_____

_____

_____

_____

_____

Note: If at any point during these 90 days of working on your spiritual growth, movement, and nutrition habits you find you are struggling to continue, just hold on! Chapters 8 and 9 are coming to offer hope and encouragement as you progress through your habit journey.

• part three •

Pressing On

"There is no fear in love, but *perfect love* casts out fear. For fear has to do with punishment, and whoever fears has not been *perfected* in love."

1 John 4:18 (ESV)

Fear, Failure, and Frustration

• chapter eight •

With my brow furrowed, tears filled my eyes. The tension in my heart matched the tightness on my face. Completely consumed by fear, no rational thought could take root. I was walking in my neighborhood, but my mind was still back at home with my teenage daughters. As I placed one foot in front of the other, my thoughts proceeded in a similar fashion. Fast, one after another. No break in my spiraling thoughts.

Parenting has brought more opportunities for fear, worry, and anxiety than anything else in my life. That particular morning, I was stuck in the fear cycle, mulling over situations that had not even occurred, practicing responses to remote possibilities, and panicking over potential problems my daughters were not even experiencing.

One stray tear rolled down my cheek and a sob escaped my mouth. My sensitive dog nudged my hand as she always does when my emotions spill over. I reached down to thank her and it was then that I caught a glimpse of the words on my t-shirt. Big, bold letters spelled out "Love > Fear.®"

Love is greater than fear.

When I bought this t-shirt from Revelation Wellness, I wasn't thinking about parenting at all. But, this morning, the source of my fear was clear. The fear I was swimming in caused me to tighten my grip on my daughters. Scary mom voice rang loudly in my mind, making me want to restrict and control their activities and assert my authority. Fear was blocking the vision God had shown me for parenting my girls. I knew that I wanted to remain connected to my daughters in their teenage years. God had led me in that direction. But fear was attempting to get in the way.

Back in Chapter 1, I shared how my loud, assertive, and controlling scary mom voice originated during a time of new parenting. Now, as fear resurfaced, so did my scary mom voice. Fear of not knowing what to do to fix the "problem" of my daughters growing up and asserting themselves. Fear screaming at me to batten down the hatches; things are out of control!

But the walking billboard on my shirt said otherwise. It said that love is greater than fear! The meaning of those words for me on this particular morning meant, "Loosen your grip on control, let go of worry, and release the outcome to God." Rather than hearing my scary mom voice rooted in fear, I heard God's voice of love. Words full of patience, hope, and grace proceeded through my mind and went straight to my heart.

Truly believing and living out the truth that love is greater than fear would draw me closer to my daughters and to God. Love over fear would result in a relaxed face, unclenched fists, and an outlook of hope. Love wouldn't focus on the right now or expect immediate change. Love would trust the process of change. It would trust that what God started, He would see through until it was good.

With my cheeks still wet with tears, I began to laugh! The irony of trekking through my neighborhood steeped in fear while wearing a Love > Fear® shirt was not lost on me. Shaking my arms, turning my head from side to side, and rolling my shoulders back, I physically released the fear. I thanked God for getting my attention and transferring my thoughts from fear onto His love.

Fear isn't the only obstacle that attempts to rob what God has for us. Fear, failure, and frustration are three roadblocks that can try to sway us from being guided in the way God is leading us. Maybe you have noticed those pesky three trying to get in the way of your progress with Grace-Filled Habits. In this chapter, we will look at how we can allow God to transform our thoughts about fear, failure, and frustration so we can continue on our merry way with our new habits.

Dear Reader, it can often feel like every possible obstacle pops up even when you have the best intentions. You intend to make changes, but fear, failure, and frustration threaten your progress at every corner. You are not alone. Let us take a good look at each of these obstacles so we can see what God has to say to us.

Fear

> "There is no fear in love, but perfect love casts out fear. For fear has to do with punishment, and whoever fears has not been perfected in love."
>
> 1 John 4:18 (ESV)

Love is the antidote for fear. In God's love, He wants to heal our thoughts in order to quiet our fear. God's love fills us with security to stifle our fear. God's love is our constant friend to shield us from fear. Just as an antidote should, God's love counteracts fear.

Has fear knocked on your door during your habit work these past few months? Have you feared that the outcome won't be what you expected?

Let's review some truths about God's character. In Chapter 2, you read about God's love and gentleness. We studied Jesus as the gentle and humble teacher, yoking with us to lighten our load. And nothing has changed. I pray that the truth about God's love and gentleness guided you in the beginning stages of developing your habits. And now that you have had experience creating and practicing habits, I pray this over you even more.

I pray that you will embrace His love for you. Hold tight to God's love, but hold loosely to your habits. Release them to God, just as you might release a person to God. In parenting, when I release my daughters to God, I get to witness His great love. We can experience that with our habits as well.

Because He cares about what we care about, we can release the outcome of our habits to Him. Fear might lead a person to weigh themselves daily or even weekly. Fear might lead a person to throw out a habit because they didn't see immediate progress. Fear might lead a person to refrain from telling someone about their new habits due to the responses they may receive.

But *there is no fear in love*. And His love *is* perfect. God, in His love, would never punish by expecting immediate outcomes, restrict more calories because the scale has not changed, or shake His head disapprovingly because a habit was missed a time or two. No. God's love keeps carrying on for the long haul.

So, Dear Reader, just as you and I are being perfected through God's love, we are also being perfected through our Grace-Filled Habits for the long haul. No immediate change required.

Friends, let's trust both the process and the outcome to God. Let's let the fear go and take hold of God's vision. Believe in His love and gentleness, which wins over fear. Quiet that scary mom voice and embrace God's voice of love!

Failure

"Therefore, since we are surrounded by so great a cloud of witnesses, let us also lay aside every weight, and sin which clings so closely, and let us run with endurance the race that is set before us."

Hebrews 12:1 (ESV)

The word "fail" sounds so final. My college history professor sure meant it as final when he marked that big fat F on my final exam. Ouch. I couldn't believe my eyes. That one grade caused me to completely rethink my choice to go to college. Could I really cut it amongst all those smart college students? Was this just the beginning of a string of academic failures?

That F seriously challenged my perfectionistic ways. Alisa Keeton, in *The Body Revelation*, shares an amazing definition of F.A.I.L—Frequent Attempts In Learning.[9] I love that. And that is exactly the experience I ended up having with my college history class. I did, in fact, fail the class. But, I also did, in fact, learn.

A year later, I took the class again. I had a different teacher with a completely different teaching style than the first professor. This new teacher held class discussions rather than lectures. This teacher assigned more essays and fewer tests. And at the end of the class this time, I walked away with a B. I passed!

In this failure, I discovered that lectures did not work well for my particular way of learning. I found that writing essays rather than answering test questions allowed me to make connections in my brain. I learned that I did not feel satisfied studying simply to earn a particular grade, but I actually wanted to benefit from the learning.

This failure taught me so much. Your failure can as well. If you will endure, you will learn and grow. If you stay the course with your Grace-Filled Habits, you will experience progress. Just as in our walk with God, we just keep plugging along. One day at a time. Some days, we see some progress, and some days we do not. It is the old saying, "It's a marathon, not a sprint!" You may have weeks or months in which you don't notice any change, improvement, or progress. But trust that you are learning.

Dear Reader, you can learn so much about yourself through your successes and failures with your habits. Have you missed some days or even weeks completing your new habits? What can you learn from the days you missed? Take note of how you felt on the days you completed your habits. Friend, get curious, not critical! Become curious about what got in the way on the days you did not complete your new habits. Get curious about what has or will bring greater success for you.

Reflection done in grace and curiosity is how you can *endure the race*, as the author of Hebrews writes in our focus verse. Getting bogged down by perceived failures will feel heavy. Beating yourself up with *shoulds* or various forms of self-criticism will feel defeating.

Imagine throwing off all the negative thoughts and self-talk around your new Grace-Filled Habits. Imagine how much lighter you will feel. Imagine being better able to see and experience your successes when you are not weighed down by that negativity.

Throughout my walk with God, I have found myself expecting much of myself. Often, I think I should be further along and should not keep falling back into an old pattern. All of these thoughts encroach on my ability to endure and only weigh me down.

Our focus verse tells us to "run with endurance the race that is set before us." So, consider that you are in a race (a long, steady race) with your habits. God has set you out on this race. Remember, you invited Him on this plan way back in Chapter 3, when you prayed and wrote your Core Value Statement. This is the race God has set before you. He's calling you to run. While you are running, He provides sustenance through endurance, patience, and grace. And He knows you will run your race the best when you "lay aside every weight, and sin which clings so closely."

Run in freedom. Let go of the idea that failure is final. Embrace the new idea of F.A.I.L—Frequent Attempts In Learning.[9] Learn away, friend! You got this!

Frustration

"For to set the mind on the flesh is death, but to set the mind on the Spirit is life and peace."

Romans 8:6 (ESV)

"I just cannot get it! I'm done!" my daughter Abby groaned in defeat. It was the day of her driver's test. All the requirements had been met: Pass the written exam—check. Turn sixteen years old—check. Schedule driving exam—check. Master parallel parking ... uh-oh.

Arriving early at the driving school for last-minute parallel parking practice seemed like a good idea. This good idea quickly turned into a terrible idea. Frustration was heavy after the fifth unsuccessful attempt. Stress filled every nook and cranny of my daughter's little Honda.

"Let's breathe," I encouraged, exaggerating my own deep inhale and exhale. Looking at the time, I saw that there was one minute until the exam. "Now let it go and I will pray you through it." My daughter exited the car and walked towards the driving school. Letting it go allowed for peace to settle over my whole body. I desired calm for Abby. A peaceful mind would perform so much better. Each failed attempt to arrive at the coveted goal of six inches away from the curb was only creating frustration. It was time to just let it go!

My flesh desired perfection. If only she could parallel park perfectly before the exam, she could have peace. But that was a lie. The goal of parking precisely six inches from the curb may not have been achievable. So, does that mean peace is just not possible in this situation? What ended up bringing peace and ultimately success (because Abby nailed parallel parking on her test) was inviting God in!

The lie of perfection is something we often fall into when we are working on our habits, but desiring perfection will only lead to frustration. Coming back to God, releasing our expectations to Him, and seeking His peace will lead to successful habits.

While the antidote for fear is love, the cure for frustration is peace. In our focus verse, Paul tells us that in order to have peace, our mind must be set on the Spirit. Contrast that with the words from our focus verse, "for to set the mind on the flesh is death."

At this point in your habit development, you could be building momentum or you could be navel-gazing, focusing inward with your mind set on your flesh. Looking for tangible, measurable, perfect results leads to death of your new habits. Alternatively, looking up, seeking God, and setting your mind on the work He is doing in and through you leads to *life and peace*.

It's time to reflect. Once again, I would like you to read your Core Value Statement. Why have you decided to develop new habits? And why are you working on these particular habits?

Some possible Core Value Statements might contain the words "increase faith," "promote health," "increase energy," or "experience more joy." None of those statements can be measured by setting your mind on your flesh. I encourage you to read your Core Value Statement to God in prayer. Then, get alone with your journal, pen, and an open heart and mind. Write down what He reveals to you. Keep asking and keep seeking. Look for how your new habits are promoting growth in your life.

Dear Reader, fear, failure, and frustration are trying to rob you of the joy of developing life-enhancing Grace-Filled Habits. But you get to fight back with God on your side. This is what makes this method of developing habits unique and powerful!

Friend, you are not alone this time! You invited God into the beginning stages of creating your new habits, and now, in this chapter, you have spent some time reflecting on His guidance. Consider fear, failure, and frustration to be weak little darts the enemy is tossing your way. Just let them fall, Dear Reader! Hold tight to God and His love for you!

Dear God, of all You offer me, I am most grateful for Your love. Your love is greater than all my fears. And Your love is what allows me to see my weaknesses as opportunities to see more of You. I ask for more of Your healing work in me so that I can more freely receive and give Your love. Amen.

Reflection Questions

How can you apply the idea that love is greater than fear to where you are at now with your Grace-Filled Habits?

_____

_____

_____

_____

_____

_____

What have you learned from your past failures?

_____

_____

_____

_____

_____

What negative self-talk can you eliminate regarding your progress with your new habits?

_____

_____

_____

_____

_____

I invite you now to write out your Core Value Statement as a prayer to God.

Example: Dear God, I give you my new habits once again. Help me develop these morning habits more fully and completely so that my ability to take care of my family and ministry responsibilities will be more fruitful.

_____

_____

_____

_____

_____

Prayer continued…

"When Jesus saw him lying there and knew that he had already been there a long time, he said to him, 'Do you want to be healed?' The sick man answered him, 'Sir, I have no one to put me into the pool when the water is stirred up, and while I am going another steps down before me.' Jesus said to him, 'Get up, take up your bed, and *walk.*' And at once the man was *healed,* and he took up his bed and walked."

John 5:6-9 (ESV)

Your Habits, Your Identity

• chapter nine •

Looking left and right, the man took note of his location. "I'm a little closer than yesterday," he mumbled under his breath. It was just as crowded as the previous days, but he thought to himself, *Maybe today will end differently*. Surrounding him were blind men, crippled women, and even children bent over in pain. Everyone looked miserable. Everyone had the same need. Everyone was waiting for their miracle.

For 38 years, his legs had failed him. Heavy and unresponsive, his legs wouldn't move when he wanted them to bear his weight, or even feel the slightest breeze pass by across his exposed ankles. They may as well not even be a part of his body. He could barely bring himself to look down at them. They were his weakness, his biggest flaw and disappointment. All-consuming thoughts about his condition ran rampant through his mind most days.

Hear Jesus whisper to you, Dear Reader, lay down your all-consuming thoughts.

Tormented by his condition, his only respite was sleep. He knew his only hope for healing was to make his way into the nearby pool because the pool held power. During certain times of the day, the water would stir up and provide the healing power he so needed. But to receive what the pool offered, he had to get into its water. And yesterday, he slept through those precious opportune minutes.

Laying on the ground, gazing at the pool, he suddenly felt an unexplainable pull to the right. Turning his head as much as he was able, he noticed a group of men walking. One of the men turned his head and met his gaze and it seemed as though this man was walking straight towards him. But surely he was imagining things. No one ever spoke to the lame man or came near to him. Others feared his condition was contagious. That is why he never got help getting into the healing pool.

Hear Jesus whisper to you, Dear Reader, to lay down your helpless status.

The lame man tried to look away from the other man's intense gaze, but he was not able. Suddenly, the man, who wore an expression of both power and kindness, spoke the strangest words. "Do you want to be healed?" he asked. "Do you want to get well?" The lame man couldn't speak and gave no response.

Do I? he thought. *I am a lame man. That is who I am. Who am I without this condition? What will be expected of me if I become well?*

The lame man summoned his voice. "Sir, I have no one to help me into the healing waters. I lay here day after day with no one to help me. Everyone else gets to the pool before me."

The man responded with more strange words. Bending down, the man extended his hand and said, "Get up! Pick up your mat, and walk!"

Hear Jesus whisper to you, Dear Reader, to lay down your old patterns.

This man is crazy! The lame man thought. *Get up? Walk? I am a lame man. That is who I am.* But, suddenly, he began to feel a tingling in his right foot. Looking down at it, he told his toes to wiggle, and they obeyed! Next thing he knew, he was rotating both ankles and wiggling all ten toes. The tingling continued all the way up his body until he could no longer contain it. The lame man sprang up onto his feet! Shifting his weight from side to side, he lifted one leg and then the other.

The man repeated to him, "Take up your sick bed and walk!"

The no-longer-lame man did as he was told. Shaking the dust off his mat, he kissed this man who told him he was no longer lame, and he walked away from that part of his life. Suddenly, he was no longer lame, helpless, or stuck. His faith in Jesus had healed him, and he was forever changed.

Who was the man who spoke healing? It was Jesus. Jesus saw the lame man's need and gave him a new identity. Jesus didn't see him as a man in need, alone, and stuck in his condition. No, Jesus saw him differently. Jesus identified the man as someone who, through faith, could get up, clean up his mess, and move on!

What about you, Dear Reader? What label have you been believing about yourself? What identity is currently holding you captive?

I have held my own share of limiting identities. In the introduction, I shared some of my health trials over the last 23 years. After my kidney transplant, I had many "come-to-Jesus" moments. Some happened in the emergency room with complications, fear, and pain, and one big clarifying moment came while lying in my bed one day feeling completely purposeless.

I had been struggling with severe migraines from the anti-rejection medications I was on following my transplant, causing me to spend a lot of time in my bed. Doctors made all the changes they were able to make, but I still felt bad most days.

After a while, I began to notice an interesting pattern. I was not in pain on days when a friend and I went on walks. Outside, I felt free. Somehow, it seemed I could leave my pain behind once I walked out of my front door. I felt purpose in moving my body and connecting with my friend. Usually, that purpose meant that I would remain free of pain even after I got home, but only for that day.

When I would awake the next morning in pain, I became so discouraged. Crying out to God from my bed one day, I asked Him the question I had been hiding. "Why would you allow me to receive this kidney transplant only to have my life be worse than before?" As I tried to slow my crying, which only made my head hurt worse, I felt His response.

His answer came straight to my heart, *Lisa, do you want to be well?*

"What? That's what I am asking for. I am asking for healing! Yes, I want to be well!"

I felt it again. *Do you really want to be well? Or are you stuck, resigned to living as a sick person?*

Oh, okay. That stopped me in my tracks. I had been sick for 18 years before my kidney transplant. Being sick was definitely part of my life. But was it my identity? And if so, was it possible to let go of that identity?

As I explained in the introduction, end-stage kidney disease came as a shock for me in my mid-twenties, and that disease remained a part of my life until my mid-forties. That was when my kidneys finally tired out completely and I had a kidney transplant. Yes, I had been sick for a long time, and I had to admit that it had become part of my identity.

But "sick person" wasn't the only identity holding me captive. I also was stuck in the belief that I was a powerless victim to everything that happened around me. I lived in my lack, never believing I was enough. All victim, no victory.

It took months of journaling, praying, and talking to friends and family about this new idea before I came to accept that having a health condition was part of my life but that it was not my identity. I accepted that bad things had happened to me and around me, but I finally understood that those things do not define me.

Little by little, I began living as a healthy person. I began living as someone who held the Holy Spirit within. I started walking a little bit each day and picking up my lightest dumbbells a few days a week. I started reading God's Word daily and journaling what He was saying to me. Slowly, I began walking in my previously overlooked identity as God's chosen daughter. I had become his healthy daughter who was ready to pick up her sickbed and walk in His calling for her life.

Dear Reader, this changed my life. Embracing a new identity will change your life as well. I am not talking about positive thinking, magical thinking, or denial. Rather, I am talking about seeking God and allowing Him to tell you and show you who you are! Friend, you are your new habits! You are a person who values the body God has given you. You are a person who seeks God with your whole life.

As I have embraced God's identity for me, I have experienced less pain. Yes, I still have a slew of medications I have to take every day to maintain my transplanted kidney. And those medications do have side effects, including painful headaches. But living in my God-given identity and purpose allows me to embrace God's power. Rather than seeing every opportunity in my life through the lens of a sick person, I can now see them as opportunities to walk in the strength God gives me.

This is the same for you, as you are also God's chosen daughter! First and foremost, you are God's child. More than being someone who lacks habits, you are God's beloved. More than being a busy mom, you are God's beloved. More than being a fast-food eater, you are God's beloved. More than being "out of shape," you are God's beloved.

Now is the time to embrace your true identity. Your true identity comes from who God is, not from anything you have done. You are God's chosen daughter because He is your Father who loves you. Powerful changes occur when you walk in your God-given identity.

In the well-known book *Atomic Habits*, author James Clear explains the science behind behavior change. He says we can change our habits at three different levels: outcomes, processes, and identity. Outcomes are focused on the end results or goals. Processes are more about changing routines. And identity is based on changing your beliefs. Clear states that identity-based habits begin with focusing on who you want to become.[10]

By taking the identity-based approach, our new identity causes our processes to change. As our processes change, our outcomes also change. Clear describes how lasting change is created. You must start believing new things about yourself and creating identity-based habits. And lasting change, Dear Reader, is what we desire!

Whether you completed all three months of your new Grace-Filled Habits or you are still working on month number one, embracing your identity now will help solidify your habits. Someone who has taken up running can now take on the identity of a runner. Someone who reads the Bible regularly can now take on the identity of being a student of the Bible. Someone who eats carrots every day can now take on the identity of a vegetable eater.

Dear Reader, practice now! Take each of your Grace-Filled Habits and write out how they can become part of your identity.

First and foremost, know that *you are God's beloved*.

Habit #1: I now regularly _____.

Thus my identity is _____.

Habit #2: I now regularly _____.

Thus my identity is _____.

Habit #3: I now regularly _____.

Thus my identity is _____.

If this feels weird or somehow untrue, go back to our focus verse. Imagine the lame man, lying on his mat next to the pool, thinking it was absurd when Jesus told him to walk. He was not currently a walking man; he was a lame man. You may not currently think of yourself as a Bible student, dedicated prayer warrior, exerciser, or vegetable eater, but God led you to your new habits, and He says otherwise!

Dear Reader, your identity is a beloved daughter of God. This means that your processes or routines are those of His beloved. Your processes are your daily habits that beautifully reflect your status as one who is guided to "take up your bed and walk." You look like someone who walks with your beloved Father. One who lays down their old identity and walks in the new. And, Dear Reader, your outcomes are coming!

Dear God, I want to be well! I need to see what I am still carrying that prevents me from receiving more of Your love, power, and healing. Thank You for meeting me right where I am. When I am lacking all motivation, You meet me with your power. When I am full of pride and ambition, You meet with your softness. You are all I need, Jesus. My faith is in You. Thank You for making me well. Amen.

Reflection Questions

What "all-consuming thoughts" have been threatening to get in the way of your God-given identity?

_____

_____

_____

_____

_____

_____

What might Jesus ask you to release or pick up so that you can walk in your identity as His beloved?

_____

_____

_____

_____

_____

_____

"Forgetting what is behind and straining towards what is *ahead*, I press on toward the goal to win the *prize* for which *God* has called me *heavenward* in Christ Jesus."

Philippians 3:13b-14 (NIV)

Moving Forward

• chapter ten •

It's a lie! You cannot actually change a habit or develop a habit in only three weeks. Whew. The pressure is off. Take a breath. If you have arrived at the end of this book and you feel like you are just getting started, you are exactly right. You are off to a wonderful start. The very definition of habit—a usual way of behaving; something that a person does often in a regular and repeated way—indicates that you will not be stopping anytime soon. Once you begin a healthy habit that enhances your life, the goal is to keep practicing it.

In her book *Cleaning Up Your Mental Mess*, Dr. Caroline Leaf explains that turning a thought into a habit takes longer. She writes that it takes about twenty-one days to create a long-term thought, but it takes about 63 days for that thought to become a habit.[11] Most experts agree that it simply takes longer than we originally thought to create a habit.

That's why I created this book, which you can use in the following ways to strengthen your new Grace-Filled Habits:

- Gather a group for accountability. Read the chapters independently and discuss the reflection questions together. Meet weekly for three months to encourage one another. Accountability fosters success.

- If you are a health coach or trainer, lead clients through this book as a three-month coaching group. Assign the chapters to be read and then discuss the reflection questions together.
- Go to www.empoweringhealthcoach.com to print out more 30-day habit trackers.

Chapter Activities and Other Coaching Suggestions

Chapter 1: What Is Getting in the Way

Coaching Tips: Have your client or group write some encouraging self-talk scripts. As they think deeper about how they would like their inner voice to sound, have them write out phrases or sentences and display them somewhere prominent in their living space (office, bedroom, etc.). Sharing these as a group is also a powerful activity. Examples: I can do hard things, I am loved and valued, and I have support.

Chapter 2: In His Gentleness and Love, God Saves

Coaching Tips: Have your client or group create a plan for rest. When and where will rest take place in their life? What will it look like? Start small! Maybe 30 minutes on a Sunday afternoon. The key is to plan it into their schedule. Ask questions about how they felt before, during, and after their rest. In a coaching group, participants should practice encouraging one another by asking how their scheduled rest time is going.

Chapter 3: Discover Your Why

Complete the Core Value exercise during your group time. Share ideas as you create your values.

Coaching Tips: Have your group share their three core values during group time. Consider setting up accountability partners or establishing accountability calls/visits with your client. The key is to notice and encourage any steps taken that match their core values.

Chapter 4: Small and Steady Wins the Race

Coaching Tips: If coaching in person, provide a mustard seed for each person you are coaching. If coaching online, Google an image of a mustard seed and share it with your clients. Next, show what the tiny seed grows into. The mustard seed is very tiny—only 1-2 millimeters in diameter—yet when fully grown, the tree can be 20-30 feet tall with branches and leaves spanning up to 20 feet wide. The magnificence of the mustard tree is not really in its height but in how wide the branches can span. Have your client(s) journal about the possibilities of their tiny Grace-Filled Habits spanning across their lives!

Chapter 5: Spiritual-Growth Habits

Coaching Tips: More 30-Day Habit Trackers can be found at www.empoweringhealthcoach.com. This is an excellent time to provide your clients with encouragement and accountability. Consider using an app such as Marco Polo to do brief check-ins, always focusing on any steps taken towards their habit. Accountability partners can ask questions such as: How did you feel on the days you completed your habit this week? What is one thing you could do today to prepare for success tomorrow?

Chapter 6: Movement Habits

Create one Grace-Filled Movement Habit and practice it along with your Spiritual-Growth Habit for 30 days.

Coaching Tips: Repeat the coaching tips for Chapter 5. Also, if you are local, plan a group walk together. Share movement ideas and utilize RevWellTV, a free resource on the Revelation Wellness website (www.revelationwellness.org), for faith-based workouts for all levels. This is also a good time to review your client's core values. How are their habits contributing to their core values?

Chapter 7: Nutrition Habits

Coaching Tips: Repeat the coaching tips for Chapter 5. If working with local clients, come together for a group meal. Create a group resource of favorite recipes to share with each other. Consider a group service project, including serving food for others in need or collecting food for a food bank.

Chapter 8: Fear, Failure, and Frustration

Coaching Tip: Share the Core Value Statement prayers as a group. Go around the group praying for one another, echoing the specific prayers.

Chapter 9: Your Habits, Your Identity

Coaching Tip: Have your group or individual client draw the outline of a person representing them. This could be done outdoors on a sidewalk or indoors on a blank sheet of paper. On the outside of the person, have them write labels or identities that get in the way of them embracing who God made them to be. Examples might include: lazy, victim, or weak. On the inside, have them write truths about their identity, including their new habits. Examples might include: chosen, God's beloved, an exerciser, or a vegetable eater.

Keep Your Momentum Going!

Dear Reader, I am so proud of all the work you have done throughout this book! You are off to a wonderful start, but remember that habits are long-term, life-long undertakings. So don't stop now! Don't lose your momentum. You want these past three months to count! And, Dear Reader, they will. Just keep going!

We all need support and encouragement while making new habits. As a faith-based health coach, I offer you just that. Imagine yourself mastering the habits you started in this book and feeling empowered to create even more life-enhancing changes. I would be honored to guide you through that process.

Let's continue this journey together! Schedule a complimentary discovery call with me to learn about my individual and group coaching programs. I am excited to listen to your story and share how we can work together to improve your overall health.

I have several methods to support you:

- One-on-one coaching
- Group coaching
- Book study groups
- Online fitness classes

Go to my website www.empoweringhealthcoach.com and click on "Schedule a Discovery Call." I look forward to meeting you!

Let's stay connected:

- Follow me on Instagram for coaching tips and encouragement: @empowering_health_
- Email me with questions: EmpHealthNW@gmail.com
- Join my Facebook Group: www.facebook.com/groups/952022745490250/
- Listen to a new podcast episode every Tuesday on the *Simple Steps for the Whole You* podcast.

God, You have been so faithful through my process of creating new habits. I ask for Your help transforming what I may have labeled as failure. Help me to press toward all that You call me to. I pray that this process of inviting You into all my habits would transform my faith and my life. Amen.

Notes

Chapter 1: What is Getting in the Way?

1. Jen Wilkin, *None Like Him*, (Wheaten, Illinois :Crossway, 2016)

Chapter 3: Discover Your Why

2. "Willpower." *Merriam-Webster.com Dictionary*, Merriam-Webster, https://www.merriam-webster.com/dictionary/willpower. Accessed 30 November 2024.
3. "New Years Resolutions Statistics 2024," *Forbes*, accessed 30 December 2023, https://www.forbes.com/health/mind/new-years-resolutions-statistics/
4. "New Years Resolutions Statistics and Trends," *drivesearch*, accessed 30 December 2023, https://www.driveresearch.com/market-research-company-blog/new-years-resolutions-statistics/

Chapter 4: Small and Steady Wins the Race

5. Stephen Guise, *Mini Habits for Weight Loss*, (Orlanda, Florida: Selective Entertainment, 2016), page 175
6. "Persistent metabolic adaptation 6 years after 'The Biggest Loser' competition," *Obesity Biology and Integrated Physiology medical journal*, accessed 12 December 2023, https://onlinelibrary.wiley.com/doi/full/10.1002/oby.21538
7. "Urgency Bias and Completion Bias: Friend or Foe to Your Productivity?", *The Harvard Business Review*, accessed 18 November 2023, https://skillpath.com/blog/urgency-bias-and-completion-bias-friend-or-foe-to-your-productivity
8. James Clear, *Atomic Habits*, (New York: Avery, 2018), page 47

Chapter 8: Fear, Failure, and Frustration

9. Alisa Keeton, *The Body Revelation*, (Carol Stream, Illinois: Tyndale, 2023)

Chapter 9: Your Habits, Your Identity

10. James Clear, *Atomic Habits*, (New York: Avery, 2018)

Chapter 10: Moving Forward

11. Dr. Caroline Leaf, *Cleaning Up Your Mental Mess*, (Ada, Michigan: Baker Books, 2021)

Acknowledgments

This book is proof that **God** is a God of miracles. When I was fourteen years old, I declared I would be a teacher and an author. I have held the desire to write for as long as I can remember. Yet, there were times in my health journey when my brain and vision were so muddled by medications that I could not fathom how I would ever be able to write a book. "You should write a book," others would say, but it seemed to be only a dream.

But God … two beautiful words. But God. He wants me to tell His story in my life, and so here it is—the first of, God-willing, more books to come!

This book is for You, God. For Your character to be made known. For Your love and gentleness have radically transformed my life. May it now transform others through Your story in my life.

To my husband, **Jeff**: Ours has been a challenging and committed relationship. And here we are, continuing to love one another and grow closer. I am so incredibly thankful for God's faithfulness shining through our marriage. You have stood by me "in sickness and in health." I cannot wait for the next twenty years, as each year just keeps getting better! My love for you continues to grow deeper and wider.

To my daughters **Mikayla and Abby**: You are my precious treasures. Life with you has been the best adventure. I have learned more from you and through you than I have through any other relationship. Your presence in my life has been my greatest gift. Thank you for always supporting me and encouraging me to dream big. I love you both to the moon and back!

To my **parents** (all four of you) and my precious **sister**: Thank you for always encouraging me as a writer and letting me "practice" health coaching with you! Thank you for always being my cheerleaders. I love you!

To my friend **Robin**: You are a gift I will never stop thanking God for. I am blessed beyond measure with the authenticity of our friendship. I love you, friend!

To my people—the ones who hire me for coaching, attend my faith and fitness classes, and come along for the ride with the Revelation Wellness book studies and programs I lead: You add so much vibrancy to my life. I am encouraged by your willingness to try new things, discuss vulnerable topics, and share so much wisdom with me. Thank you for being my people!

To **Michelle Tornetta**, my amazing podcast partner: God brought us together to encourage women, and I cannot wait to see where He continues to lead. I love creating Simple Steps for the Whole You with you!

To my book coach, **Alyson Rockhold**: Your encouragement and teaching have led me to complete my first book. Not only that, it has led me to desire to write more! I couldn't have asked for more. Thank you!

In memory of **Emily Locke**, my beautiful kidney donor. Learning of the bold way in which she loved and lived has forever transformed my life. I cannot wait to hug her in heaven. Emily and her family's selfless love is why there is a book titled, *Grace-Filled Habits*. God bless you, **Locke family**.

About the Author

Lisa Ostreim is a follower and beloved daughter of Jesus. After teaching children for twenty years, Lisa transitioned to coaching women. Lisa received her training and certifications through the Institute for Integrative Nutrition and Revelation Wellness. She applies Biblical truths as she coaches individuals and groups in the areas of health and fitness. Lisa teaches online and in-person fitness classes designed for all levels and is highly invested in her local Revelation Wellness community, serving as a Regional Captain. Lisa helps co-host the *Simple Steps for the Whole You* podcast on all major podcast platforms. Her desire is for others to come to know how very loved and cherished they are by God.

Lisa lives in Washington State with her husband, Jeff, and their two teenage daughters, Mikayla and Abby. She enjoys reading, walking, hiking, and strength training. Lisa is passionate about her community of women who are on mission to get and stay free.

Made in the USA
Columbia, SC
29 April 2024

34787521R00080